How To Play
WINNING
BLACKJACK

by Julian H. Braun, M.S.

DATA HOUSE PUBLISHING CO. INC. 7525 N. Wolcott Ave. • Chicago, IL 60626 • 312/973-5109

DATA HOUSE

First Edition 1980
Second Printing 1980
©Copyright 1980 by
Data House Publishing Co., Inc.

Data House Publishing Co., Inc.
7525 No. Wolcott Avenue
Chicago, IL. 60626

Printed in the
United States of America

Library of Congress Catalog
Card No. 79-56327
ISBN-0-935-822-00-3

FOREWORD

I have several reasons for writing this book. First and foremost, is that some of the ideas and observations contained may be of benefit to the hundreds of thousands of Blackjack players who have been or will become as devoted or intrigued with the game as I am.

Secondly, since my name and work in the field have been quoted in over a dozen books and in countless articles, this is an attempt to correct, clarify, and at the very least, to amplify my findings so as to clear up any misunderstandings.

The reader should be forewarned that I am neither a raconteur or even an ex-pit boss (heaven forbid). Accordingly, and unlike some other books on the subject, you will find none of the pithy, and sometimes very enjoyable "insider" stories about the colorful cast of characters who exist on the fringe of both sides of the table.

Rather, I shall attempt as logically as possible to trace for you my work over the past 18 years. In so doing, it will help crystalize and support the foundation of the Basic Strategy charts contained, particularly in the area of the four or six deck games.

Along the way, we shall also closely examine many of the dilemmas one often encounters such as the Double 8 vs. the Ten, or the hard 13 vs. the 7. Finally, I will have some observations about many of the systems being offered, about systems in general, and will introduce my own Point-Count strategy.

My research in Blackjack continues to be a pleasant avocation for me. I sincerely hope this book proves valuable and profitable to you.

Julian H. Braun
Chicago
1980

TABLE OF CONTENTS

Introduction

LIST OF CHARTS

INTRODUCTION

Las Vegas has changed dramatically since I first visited it in 1958. Today's Strip is a never to be forgotten impact on the senses which has to be seen to be believed. Each hotel and casino along the way vies to light up its own share of the Las Vegas sky with vivid pinks, blues and greens. Star-studded attractions beckon in all directions. Fine chefs prepare every kind of ethnic food imaginable, and excellent shopping abounds. Las Vegas' neighbors to the North, Reno and Tahoe, are each enjoying robust growth. Reno is expanding to a strip of its own and Tahoe is burgeoning in the natural beauty of its Lake, its woodlands, and its ski slopes.

And now, Atlantic City. The grand old Boardwalk will never be the same. New casinos are opening almost daily, with many more under construction. And the influx of super-star performers and gourmet chefs are giving this old resort city the aura of an East coast Las Vegas. Head South to the Bahamas. From the great native Market in downtown Nassau, it is just a short walk to the bridge leading to beautiful Paradise Island. What a combination! The tranquil Atlantic during the day and a beautiful casino at night. Continue South to the great islands of the Carribean, Puerto Rico, Curacao, Haiti, Martinique, St. Martin and Aruba.

Want a change to something just a little more sophisticated? In London, walk a few blocks from Buckingham Palace to the elegant mini-casinos. Here you'll be greeted royally by formally attired men and women. You'll dine splendidly on continental food in picturesque and intimate surroundings. Cross the channel to Ostend, then on to Baden-Baden (perhaps the most beautiful casino in the world), and famous Monte Carlo. Or would you prefer Djakarta or Macao? The list continues to grow each year.

There is, of course, the one super attraction all these casinos have in common. The gambling phenomenon known the world round as Blackjack (Vingt et un in France). It's evolvement as the world's most popular gambling game has been nothing short of sensational. I have long pondered over its success. Several factors apparently contribute. The first of these is it combines skill with chance. You don't just simply sit there and wait for a little ball to drop into a slot. Instead, you are a genuine participant. Your decisions materially affect the outcome. It also possesses a kind of gentility. You sit comfortably, and almost socially, alongside your co-players. The Dealer, more often than not a congenial sort of person, acts more like a friendly referee rather than a foe. Add to this the superficial simplicity of the game and the experience becomes a pleasant one. Finally, the more liberalized rules, especially in Las Vegas and Atlantic City, appeal to the winner in all of us. And truly, it is quite possible to win at Blackjack, fairly and squarely. The hows and ways to accomplish this are what this book is all about.

So here it is, the Casino World. For most people, it's a long-weekend kind of world. Appealing, because it combines fine entertainment, activities like swimming, hiking, sightseeing, shopping, fine dining, and the excitement and challenge of the Casino.

A word of caution. The information in this book is to enlighten you in the ways of the game. The very meaning of the word "gambling," means you can win or you can lose. We take no responsibility or credit for either. Play smart, play tough, and go with luck.

This book is dedicated to that vast group of men and women who share with me that special exuberance for the game of Blackjack, and for whom I hope this book shall prove incalculably rewarding.

1

HOW TO APPROACH THE GAME

At the very beginning, I asked my publisher what seemed to be a simple question. "What kind of people are going to read this book?" I suppose I was looking for a pat answer, one that would draw a straight line for me, from here to there. After all, I am a mathematician, and we have a way of thinking in straight lines. Instead of the pat answer I expected, I received this one.

"You would be between 21 and 80 and be male or female. You might never have played Blackjack before or played once or twice. You may even have been playing for years. You might be conservative by nature or flamboyant, or somewhere in between. Your math might be very good or just so-so. Your interest in the game might be casual or serious. You might want to win or lose a few dollars or a few hundred." Now, with a profile like this, go write a straight line kind of book. I certainly hope you can find yourself somewhere in the above description. If not, I'm out of luck.

Seriously, my objective is to be meaningful to all my readers. This means the more advanced players may wish to skip the basics. But be careful. It's really not a bad idea to review. Maybe you'll see something you've missed.

The book will proceed in this manner. The first chapter will deal with the fundamentals of the game; the rules, procedures, objectives and definitions. From that beginning, we'll immediately progress into the Basic Strategy for four decks. Here indeed you will gain the knowledge you must absolutely possess if you hope to play the house even, and to have a good chance of winning. Every move, every condition will be carefully exposed to provide you with the background necessary to make sound decisions. We will then take a look at the guts of the game, the interaction between you and it. We'll examine words like intuition, luck and skill, and the tremendously important part you play in the game.

Finally I will detail the Braun Count System, never before published; and share with you some of my observations of other systems being offered.

As we walk into the Casino, a few words to think about. You are your own master. You can play as little or as long as you like, and bet as little or as much as you want. You can quit as simply as standing up. The experience can run the gamut from being fun and adventurous to being extremely uncomfortable. Just be good to yourself, and walk away when it isn't fun anymore.

RULES OF THE GAME

For those of you unfamiliar with the rules of Blackjack, the game is played on a semi-circular table covered in a green or blue felt. The table is marked as shown in the diagram on the next page. The seven squares represent the player positions. The right angle box on the inside left end is for storage of the played cards. The larger area immediately in front of the

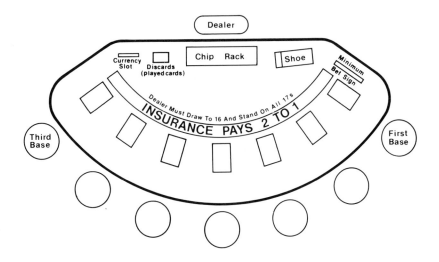

dealer is the repository for the Dealer's supply of chips. The square box on the right hand side represents the "shoe" from which the Dealer passes the cards to each of the players and to himself. The narrow rectangular sign to the extreme right is used to announce the minimum bet which is accepted at the table. Although you may find $1.00 minimums "downtown," most casinos now have a $2.00 minimum. Inflation, you know. Other minimums you will see posted are $5, $10, $25 and $100. You will occasionally see a Reserved sign. These are for the very large bettors who will many times play 3 or 4 positions. The maximum bet in most of the larger United States casinos is either $500 or $1,000.

Since much of what you will be learning depends upon the rules of play for the particular casino, it is a good idea to obtain a copy of these rules before you start. A printed sheet or folder can often be procured at the cashier's cage. Spend a few minutes with these rules before you begin. Such questions as to whether you can double down on any two cards or after a split are very important.

HOW YOU BET

The medium for betting is usually chips. These are of high quality plastic, engraved or decorated with the casino name. Denominations most frequently are $1.00, $5.00, $25.00 and $100.00. These are given to you in exchange for your money at the Cashier's cage. You may also get them right at the table, though you must go to the Cashier to cash in your chips. The major casinos in Las Vegas do have an exchange of chips agreement.* Not infrequently you will find cash being used for the bet. This is acceptable; however, you will be paid in chips should you win your bet.

THE SHUFFLE

The dealer shuffles the cards and offers them to one of the players along with a plastic indicator card which the player inserts anywhere in the deck. This performs the function of a "cut." After cutting, the Dealer places this indicator approximately one-fourth of the way from the end. It will signify the end of that particular "shoe" when he gets to it, and the Dealer will reshuffle. He then proceeds to "burn" the first card, placing it in the played cards box. He then deals a card to each player in turn, including himself beginning at his left, and then a second card in the same manner. After finishing this ritual, the Dealer exposes one of his cards for all to see.

> *Some casinos in the U.S., and particularly in Europe are now dealing all cards face up with the exception, of course, of the Dealer's down or hole card. This has been distressing to those people who feel as though they are giving up something, or even being cheated.*
>
> *They miss the adventure of "peeking" at their cards when they come. Personally, I prefer the cards up. It is a much*

---

* This exchange has been curtailed of late.

12

faster game since you never even touch the cards. As far as giving up anything, that is simply not true since there is no reason for you to hide anything from the Dealer. We'll cover this in greater detail when we describe the Dealer's function. Suffice it to say at this point, the cards being dealt face up or down have absolutely no effect on the outcome of the game.

Another new development which does have a greater impact is when the Dealer does not take his hole card until after all the hands have been played. This will be discussed in greater detail in our chapter on "Surrender."

CARD VALUES

Each of the cards in the deck has a numerical value. The numbered cards deuce (2) through ten (10) carry their face value. All picture cards, Jack, Queen, King, carry a value of ten. Since all ten valued cards are treated equivalently, whenever the term "ten" is used in this book for a single card, it should be taken to mean "any ten valued card." Aces may be counted as one or eleven.

OBJECTIVE OF THE GAME

You will have won your bet when the total amount of all your cards is greater than that of the Dealer, providing you have not exceeded 21. If your count has exceeded 21, you have gone "Bust," and you are an automatic loser regardless of whether the Dealer also goes "Bust" at some subsequent time. You will also have lost your bet if the Dealer's count is greater than yours. Another way you will win your bet is for you to "stand" with your count and for the Dealer to go "Bust." When both your count and that of the Dealer are the same (a tie) then no one is con-

sidered to be the winner, and no money changes hands. This is known as a
"push."

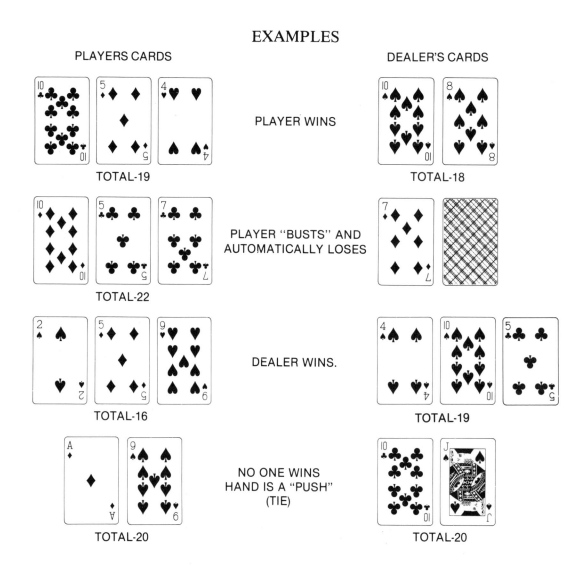

EXAMPLES

PLAYERS CARDS   DEALER'S CARDS

PLAYER WINS

TOTAL-19   TOTAL-18

PLAYER "BUSTS" AND
AUTOMATICALLY LOSES

TOTAL-22

DEALER WINS.

TOTAL-16   TOTAL-19

NO ONE WINS
HAND IS A "PUSH"
(TIE)

TOTAL-20   TOTAL-20

*THE GREAT HOUSE ADVANTAGE: It is obvious from
the above you can "hit" your hand at any time. That is,
you can ask the Dealer to give you another card. You will
be "hitting" in this manner many times when you are in a
position to bust (go over 21). Should you do so, and the*

*Dealer also busts when it comes his turn to hit, it will be to
no avail since he will have already taken your chips. It is
this fact that constitutes the great House Advantage.
Knowing this, the tendency of some people is not to hit for
fear of busting. Never hit, never bust. This is a totally er-
roneous conclusion which will be shown as we proceed.*

THE DEALER AND SEVENTEEN

As a player, you have the option of hitting your hand or staying with the
cards you have. The Dealer has no such option. The rules for his play are
established, and he can not willfully change those rules. The most important of these is that the Dealer must hit his hand up to and including sixteen. He must stand on seventeen. There is an important difference between casinos of which you should be aware. In most major casinos in the
U.S., the Dealer must stand on any 17, soft or hard, i.e. A-6 or 10-7. Most
casinos in Reno, the casinos in downtown Las Vegas and many smaller
casinos located elsewhere, as well as some in Europe, require the Dealer to
hit his soft seventeen (A,6 or A,2,4 or A,3,3, etc.). Unfortunately, the latter provides the house with an extra advantage of about one fifth of a percent. If you have your choice, choose the casino that stops at seventeen,
soft or hard.

SIGNALS YOU SHOULD LEARN

There is usually very little conversation which occurs between the players
and the Dealer. It is not disallowed, but the game moves so swiftly, that
signals or signs are used to communicate. These differ slightly depending
on whether the cards are dealt face up or down. With face down, you show
your desire to stay (stand) by sliding the two cards under the chips you have

bet (placed in your square). The Dealer will now pass you by when it comes your turn. Contrarily, when you wish to be "hit" (another card) you brush your two cards against the table motioning toward yourself. You continue this motioning until you wish to stay (receive no more cards). At this point, you place your first two closed cards under the chips. In the instance of the open game, you never touch the cards. Instead, you signal your "hit" desire by tapping the table with your finger at a point adjacent to your cards. To stay, place your hand over and parallel to your cards and move it left to right, as if to say "no more".

OPEN GAME—CLOSED GAME: A number of casinos in the U.S. have switched to dealing your cards face up. This practice is very prevalent in European casinos. They have two reasons for doing so. It materially speeds up the game since none of the players ever touch the cards. And since the house (casino) believes they will win the greater percentage of hands, it is to their advantage to have more hands dealt during the course of any given hour. The second reason is to foil the potential cheater who has perfected ways of either marking (daubing) or crimping the cards. The open game does have some advantages to you as a player. I have seen innumerable instances where for one reason or another the player has miscounted. The Dealer will almost always save you from yourself. The open game also makes it a little easier to "count" the cards if you are using some type of system.

SLOWING DOWN THE FAST DEALER: Some Dealers, for reasons of their own, enjoy their "control" of the pace of the game. It is amazing how quickly they can deal. Such a Dealer can be very intimidating to either the novice or even to the seasoned player who must take a little longer to add the total of his cards. Don't let this happen to you. You are the "customer" so to speak. Take as much time as you need. There is no way they can go past you; it is simply not allowed. So take the time you need. The Dealer will soon learn you will not be intimidated, and will slow down the game accordingly.

SIGNALING A BLACK JACK

You will be dealt a blackjack (Ace and ten) in your first two cards about 5 times in every one hundred hands. You signal this fact in the closed cards game by waiting for your turn, and then revealing both cards by placing them face up to the front of your chips and toward the Dealer. He will automatically pay you three chips for every two you have bet.

WHAT IF DEALER ALSO HAS A BLACKJACK: Most casinos require the Dealer to look at his "hole" (face down) card whenever his open card is either an ace or a ten value card. His purpose for doing so is to see if he has a blackjack. In that instance when his up card is an Ace, he will ask, "Insurance?" (The subject of Insurance will be covered in full in a subsequent chapter.) For the moment, assume that even with your blackjack you do not take insurance. If he does indeed have the blackjack he will turn his card over to show that fact to the players. He will then uncover the players' cards in turn. When he turns your cards and sees your blackjack, he will signal a "push" meaning a tie, and no chips will change hands. The same is

true were his up card a ten. The only difference is the offer
for insurance is not made. If in fact he does not have a
blackjack, then the game proceeds in the typical manner
with you revealing your blackjack when your turn comes.

SIGNALING THE DOUBLE DOWN

All casinos in the United States permit you to ''Double Down'' when the value of your first two cards is ten or eleven. Many casinos, notably those in Las Vegas, allow the double down on any two cards. Since you will have a worthwhile double down opportunity approximately ten times out of every one hundred hands, the strategy for doing so is of extreme importance. The chapter on Double Downs will completely examine this subject. You signal the double down by turning your cards face up and placing them to the front of your chips. At the same time, you place the same amount of chips as your original bet adjacent to your chips. You will receive only one additional card when doubling down.

SIGNALING SPLITTING OF PAIRS

All casinos permit you to ''split'' pairs when you receive such in your first two cards. Most also permit you a third split and even a fourth split should your hit be the same value as the pair you split. (Except in a few generous casinos, the usual rule is that aces may not be resplit whereas other pairs may be resplit up to a maximum of 4 resultant hands). Splitting pairs is a very important part of the game. Strategy for this option will be discussed in its own chapter. You signal your desire to split the pair by revealing your cards and placing one of the cards to the left of your wagered chips, and the other to the right. You further place the same amount of chips as your original bet alongside your original chips. You will now be playing two separate hands with each of the values of your pair.* They no longer

---

* When splitting aces, you will receive only one card for each ace in most casinos.

have any relationship to each other. Instead, the outcome is predicated upon what happens to each. NOTE: In almost all casinos any two ten valued cards can be regarded as a pair. For example, if you get a Jack and a King you have a pair which may be split. This particular move however, is never recommended unless you are using a count system.

It is possible for you to play more than one position providing the position next to you on either side is not occupied. In order to do so, you must, in most casinos, wager at least twice the minimum of that table for each position. i.e. at a five dollar minimum table, your bet at each position must be at least ten dollars.

We have completed the basic rules and etiquette for playing Blackjack. We can now begin.

2

YOUR BEST MOVES: A BASIC STRATEGY

Did you ever wonder why in almost every profession there are people or groups who seem to succeed most of the time? Whether it be a particular film producer or business corporation or novelist or sports star, they somehow win more often than not.

My guess is that behind each of these successes is a planned approach, a basic strategy if you will, that through trial and error has proven right. What has inevitably followed with such individuals has been a consistency and faithfulness to their strategy so as to produce a continuity of successful results.

All of this is by way of introducing you to the Basic Strategy of Blackjack. The trial and error is represented by the millions of computer results which show what your best move under each specific condition should be. Does that mean you will win every time? The answer is no. First of all, Basic Strategy only allows you to play the house about even. Next, even the people referred to above lose some of the time.

I happen to be writing this chapter the day after the 1979 U.S. Open. Chris Evert Lloyd was seeking her fifth consecutive championship. She did not get it. She lost to Tracy Austin. Does that mean Chris' Basic Strategy was wrong? How can any one possibly say that. What a brilliant winning record she has compiled! That day it did not work. She was a loser. But does that negate the hundreds of matches and dozens of championships she did win with her Basic Strategy?

I personally know of no one who wins all of the time. I know many who win most of the time. I also know many who lose most of the time. Consistency and belief in your Basic Strategy is the only answer.

Unfortunately, there are many flukes that pay off; random hunches that result in a big winner, and intuitions that ring the bell. Each of these tend to obscure and undermine the idea of consistency. I have no quarrel with intuition. Look, if you had a dream last night that 14 candles were flickering to the tune of The Lady in Red, then for heaven's sake put $50.00 down on 14 Red at the roulette table and get it out of your system. Just don't try it at the Blackjack table.

May I tell you what's wrong with hunches? Let's assume you will be playing for an hour or two at a time, and that you will be doing so on several occasions each of the days you are there. During that time you will be dealt hundreds of hands, and it is safe to assume, you will have dozens of hunches or intuitions. I can guarantee you will win some and lose the others. Pretty soon you will be asking, "will the real hunch please stand up?" It simply won't work.

Winning at Blackjack demands a game plan. Something you can believe in and be guided by. Basic Strategy is at the foundation of it all. You must adhere to it strictly, deviating not at all. Your moves must be as mechanical as those of the Dealer.

There are three basic elements we will now begin considering. The first of these is the actual play, that is when to bet, stand, double down or split. Next will be the important aspect of money management. Finally, how to make the decision whether to continue playing or to quit.

BASIC STRATEGY: NUMBERS TO LIVE BY

As you've guessed by now, I've had some fun with the computer during the past eighteen years. But when I had finished with the multitude of computations, the result was the deceptively simple chart of recommendations shown on the next page.

It is important for you to thoroughly understand this chart. You have several options for doing so. You may learn it by rote. That is, you can put it to memory without going any deeper. Or you may wish to examine each of the actions to see why the particular decision is made. I strongly urge you to take on the second course. I will try to give you some incentive for doing so.

It has been my experience that understanding is a far more reliable ally to the memory than is sheer repetition. For example, you can learn through repetition that you should double down when you have A,6 and the Dealer's face card is a 5. It is a fact of the chart that you can work at remembering along with the dozens of other facts you must learn. On the other hand, if you turn to the illustrated Strategy page for a soft count of 17 (in the double-down chapter) and see that of every hundred times you

CHART NO. 1

BASIC STRATEGY FOR FOUR OR MORE DECKS

DEALER SHOWS

YOUR HAND	2	3	4	5	6	7	8	9	10	ACE
8	H	H	H	H	H	H	H	H	H	H
9	H	D	D	D	D	H	H	H	H	H
10	D	D	D	D	D	D	D	D	H	H
11	D	D	D	D	D	D	D	D	D	H
12	H	H	S	S	S	H	H	H	H	H
13	S	S	S	S	S	H	H	H	H	H
14	S	S	S	S	S	H	H	H	H	H
15	S	S	S	S	S	H	H	H	H	H
16	S	S	S	S	S	H	H	H	H	H
A,2	H	H	H	D	D	H	H	H	H	H
A,3	H	H	H	D	D	H	H	H	H	H
A,4	H	H	D	D	D	H	H	H	H	H
A,5	H	H	D	D	D	H	H	H	H	H
A,6	H	D	D	D	D	H	H	H	H	H
A,7	S	D	D	D	D	S	S	H	H	H
A,8	S	S	S	S	S	S	S	S	S	S
A,9	S	S	S	S	S	S	S	S	S	S
A,A	SP	SP	SP	SP	SP	SP	SP	SP	SP	SP
2,2	H	H	SP	SP	SP	SP	H	H	H	H
3,3	H	H	SP	SP	SP	SP	H	H	H	H
4,4	H	H	H	H	H	H	H	H	H	H
6,6	H	SP	SP	SP	SP	H	H	H	H	H
7,7	SP	SP	SP	SP	SP	SP	H	H	H	H
8,8	SP	SP	SP	SP	SP	SP	SP	SP	SP	SP
9,9	SP	SP	SP	SP	SP	S	SP	SP	S	S
10,10	S	S	S	S	S	S	S	S	S	S

H = HIT   S = STAND   D = DOUBLE DOWN   SP = SPLIT PAIRS

have A,6 vs. 5, the probabilities are that you will win 10 more hands than you will lose in every 100, or an advantage of 10% in favor of doubling compared to hitting. The "fact" is fortified by comprehension. (For further clarification see the section on the Mathematics of Doubling Down in Chapter 3.)

It is this understanding that reinforces the memory. Beyond that is the incentive of confidence - the important feeling you are doing the right thing. In the example given above, the probability is you will win 55% of the time and lose 45%. You are playing with the odds on your side. You are not just following some chart on faith.

The final incentive is our old friend, money. The bottom line. I am a firm believer that understanding promotes winning ... and consolation when you are losing. Let's face it, each of us can be a great winner but how many can be a consoled loser? I really don't mean this to be funny. The probability is that overall, you are going to lose half the time when you play four-deck Blackjack. The consolation is that you know it; and therefore you won't be surprised when it happens. This is a roundabout way of having you keep your cool, keep your game plan, and thus have a good shot at winning.

Back to the chart. Choose your own way, but learn it. This is what you paid for, and you will be coming back to it a hundred times.

The symbols used throughout this report are as follows:

H	S	D	SP	G
Hit	Stand	Double Down	Split Pairs	Surrender (Give Up)

The numbers shown vertically represent the total of your cards, or your pairs, or Ace with additional card.

Please spend a little time with Chart No. 1 right now to be sure you understand the recommendation for each play. Notice as you study it represents every conceivable condition which can occur in the game of Blackjack.

THE 12 TO 17 DILEMMA

In a forthcoming chapter on Good Hands - Bad Hands, we state you will be getting a hard 12 to 17 about 43% of the time. Further, the only way you could possibly win with such a hand was to either improve it or have the Dealer bust.

The recommended actions for counts of 12 - 17 are shown on Chart No. 1. We are about to examine in detail each of these totals to understand why we hit or stand.

> *More players stumble on the hard counts of 12 - 17 than any other. Let's face it, they are terrible hands. They make us uncomfortable, and they cost us money. We're afraid to hit for fear of busting. We're afraid to stand for fear the Dealer will show a better count. It is precisely for these reasons we must learn how to minimize their terrible consequences.*

In considering those combinations which add up to either 8, 12, 14 or 16, the paired 4, the paired 6, the paired 7 and the paired 8 have been omitted for later discussion in the Chapter on Splitting Pairs.

Each of the count pages which follow illustrate the probabilities of hitting or standing with each of the counts being considered against each of the Dealer's face up cards.* The box score underneath each possible Dealer's face-up card shows the percentage gained as a result of your best option in comparison with the second best option. For example, in determining what you should do when you have a total of 12 and the Dealer's face up card is a deuce, it tells you the following. Based on 100 hands, by hitting your 12 you would win 37 times and lose 63. By standing, you would win 35 hands and lose 65. You can see from these probabilities that while your 12 is a losing hand overall, you will lose 2 less hands by hitting. This shows up as a +4 for hitting. (All data has been compiled to 4 decimal places for accuracy. Rounding to the nearest percent can result in some figures which may look slightly off.) The +4 referred to above is a percentage gain. Suppose you had bet just $1 on each hand. If you hit, your result averages plus $37 minus $63 for a net loss of $26. If you stand, your result averages plus $35 minus $65 for a net loss of $30. Thus you gain $4 or 4% of the money wagered by hitting rather than standing.

Therefore, the recap on the 12 count page, as well as Chart No. 1 recommends you hit your 12 when the Dealer has a 2 showing.

Please recognize that your total of 12 may come from more than two cards. For example, your first two cards are 4 - 3. You hit and receive a 5. Your total is now 12 and the strategy above now prevails.

Notice that there is not a single case where a holding of 12 to 17 has a win probability exceeding 50%. More often than not it is a losing hand. In each case the choice of hitting or standing is chosen for the purpose of losing less.

---

*Unless otherwise indicated the data shown is for the four-deck game. I have run the six-deck game through the computer and find no significant differences from four-deck strategy.

I repeat a portion of the last sentence. "...for the purpose of losing less." I must tell you this phrase is half the secret. The other half is "winning more." I hope the implications are clear. You will have your share of stiffs. If you can find a way to lose less of those than otherwise, the "less" becomes a gain. Contrarily, you will have your share of winning hands. If you can find a way of "winning more" when you do have such winning hands that too is a gain. It is the ability to play for these extra gains that makes for a tough and successful player.

HOW TO PLAY THE HARD COUNTS OF 12 TO 17 IN A SINGLE DECK GAME.

The correct basic strategy is essentially the same as for the four deck game except for some very minor differences. In general, you should stand with 16 against a 10 if the 16 is made up of 3 or more cards. With a holding of (10,3) or (10,2,A) hit against a dealer 2. It is of very little consequence if you do not remember these differences as the increased gain by using them is quite small.

There exist some other very minor differences for various 3 or more card holdings, but it would be tedious to list these and even more tedious to commit them to memory. The potential gain is exceedingly small.

DEALER SHOWS

	W	L
H	37	63
S	35	65
H	+4	

	W	L
H	38	62
S	37	63
H	+2	

	W	L
H	40	60
S	40	60
S	+0	

	W	L
H	40	60
S	42	58
S	+3	

	W	L
H	41	59
S	42	58
S	+2	

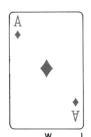

	W	L
H	39	61
S	28	72
H	+22	

	W	L
H	36	64
S	26	74
H	+20	

	W	L
H	33	67
S	24	76
H	+17	

	W	L
H	31	69
S	24	76
H	+14	

	W	L
H	32	68
S	20	80
H	+25	

YOUR CARDS

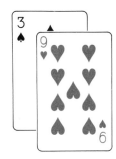
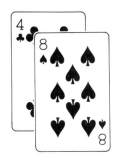

RECAP

	2	3	4	5	6	7	8	9	10	A
	H	H	S	S	S	H	H	H	H	H
12	+4	+2	+0	+3	+2	+22	+20	+17	+14	+25

COMMENTS

Hit a 12 except when dealer shows a 4, 5, or 6. Note that the relative gain for standing on 12 when the dealer shows a 4 is shown as +0. Actually, it is —.04% for a holding at 10,2 and +1% for the other two card 12's. The properly weighted average is a shade over +0. A fine point of basic strategy is to hit a 10,2 versus a dealer 4, but if you do not use this fine point the difference is negligible.

29

13

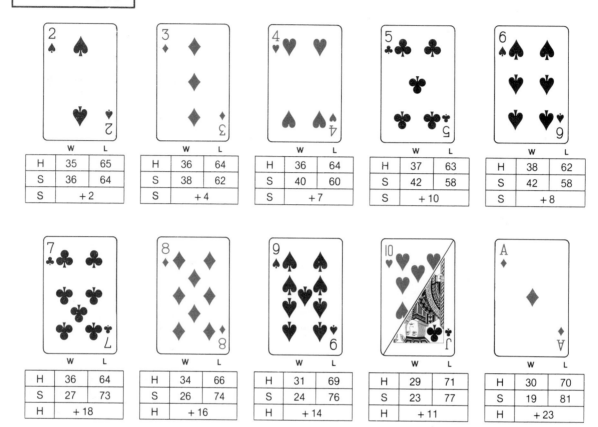

	W	L
H	35	65
S	36	64
S	+2	

	W	L
H	36	64
S	38	62
S	+4	

	W	L
H	36	64
S	40	60
S	+7	

	W	L
H	37	63
S	42	58
S	+10	

	W	L
H	38	62
S	42	58
S	+8	

	W	L
H	36	64
S	27	73
H	+18	

	W	L
H	34	66
S	26	74
H	+16	

	W	L
H	31	69
S	24	76
H	+14	

	W	L
H	29	71
S	23	77
H	+11	

	W	L
H	30	70
S	19	81
H	+23	

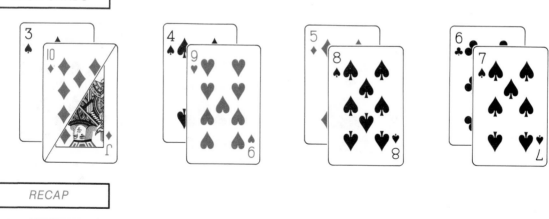

	2	3	4	5	6	7	8	9	10	A
13	S	S	S	S	S	H	H	H	H	H
	+2	+4	+7	+10	+8	+18	+16	+14	+11	+23

An undesirable hand! Stand if the dealer shows 6 or less and hope that he busts. Hit if the dealer shows 7 or better until you get 17 or more. You will still likely lose but will lose less on average.

	W	L
H	32	68
S	36	64
S	+7	

	W	L
H	33	67
S	38	62
S	+10	

	W	L
H	33	67
S	40	60
S	+13	

	W	L
H	34	66
S	42	58
S	+16	

	W	L
H	35	65
S	42	58
S	+15	

	W	L
H	34	66
S	27	73
H	+14	

	W	L
H	32	68
S	25	75
H	+13	

	W	L
H	28	72
S	23	77
H	+10	

	W	L
H	27	73
S	23	77
H	+7	

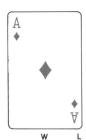

	W	L
H	28	72
S	18	82
H	+20	

YOUR CARDS

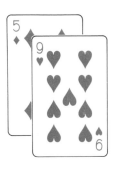

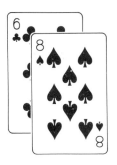

RECAP

	2	3	4	5	6	7	8	9	10	A
14	S	S	S	S	S	H	H	H	H	H
	+7	+10	+13	+16	+15	+14	+13	+10	+7	+20

COMMENTS

A bad hand! Stand if the dealer shows 6 or less and hope that he busts. Hit if the dealer shows 7 or better until you get 17 or more. You will likely lose but will lose less on average.

DEALER SHOWS

	W	L
H	29	71
S	35	65
S	+13	

	W	L
H	30	70
S	38	62
S	+16	

	W	L
H	30	70
S	40	60
S	+20	

	W	L
H	31	69
S	42	58
S	+23	

	W	L
H	31	69
S	42	58
S	+22	

	W	L
H	32	68
S	27	73
H	+10	

	W	L
H	29	71
S	24	76
H	+9	

	W	L
H	26	74
S	23	77
H	+7	

	W	L
H	25	75
S	23	77
H	+4	
G	*	

	W	L
H	26	74
S	17	83
H	+17	

YOUR CARDS

  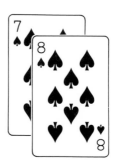

RECAP

	2	3	4	5	6	7	8	9	10	A
15	S	S	S	S	S	H	H	H	H	H
	+13	+16	+20	+23	+22	+10	+9	+7	+4	+17

COMMENTS

A terrible hand! Stand if the dealer shows 6 or less and hope that he busts. Hit if the dealer shows 7 or better until you get 17 or more. You will still likely lose but lose less on average. *If you are allowed to surrender (see later chapter) you may achieve a small gain doing so with holdings of (10, 5) or (9, 6) against a dealer ten.

	W	L
H	27	73
S	35	65
S	+18	

	W	L
H	27	73
S	37	63
S	+21	

	W	L
H	29	71
S	40	60
S	+23	

	W	L
H	28	72
S	42	58
S	+29	

	W	L
H	29	71
S	42	58
S	+26	

    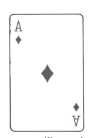

	W	L
H	30	70
S	26	74
H	+7	

	W	L
H	27	73
S	24	76
H	+6	

	W	L
H	25	75
S	23	77
H	+4	
G	+.2	

	W	L
H	23.4	76.6
S	22.8	77.2
H	+.8	
G	+3	

	W	L
H	24	76
S	17	83
H	+15	
G	+1	

 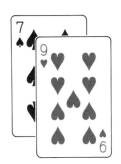

	2	3	4	5	6	7	8	9	10	A
16	S	S	S	S	S	H	H	H	H	H
	+18	+21	+23	+29	+26	+7	+6	+4	+.8	+15

The worst possible hand you can get! Stand if the dealer shows 2 to 6 and hope that the dealer busts. Hit if the dealer shows a 7 or better. You will still likely lose but will lose less on average. If surrender is permitted (see later chapter!) do so against a dealer 9, 10 or ace.

	W	L
H	23	77
S	42	58
S	+38	

	W	L
H	23	77
S	44	56
S	+42	

	W	L
H	24	76
S	46	54
S	+45	

	W	L
H	24	76
S	48	52
S	+47	

	W	L
H	24	76
S	50	50
S	+51	

	W	L
H	26	74
S	44	56
S	+36	

	W	L
H	25	75
S	31	69
S	+11	

	W	L
H	23	77
S	29	71
S	+13	

	W	L
H	21	79
S	29	71
S	+16	

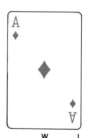

	W	L
H	22	78
S	26	74
S	+18	

 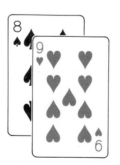

	2	3	4	5	6	7	8	9	10	A
17	S	S	S	S	S	S	S	S	S	S
	+38	+42	+45	+47	+51	+36	+11	+13	+16	+8

Always stand on a hard count of 17 or more. A hard count of 17 is not a particularly good hand, but hitting it would lose more.

3

THE IMPORTANCE OF DOUBLING DOWN

In the preceding chapter we discussed your alternatives for the counts of 12 thru 17. Your first thought must have been what terrible hands these are, and you are right. You get them too often, and lose too many.

You may have wondered right then and there how you could possibly play the house even, let alone win. Well, this chapter and the next on splitting pairs are good parts of the answer. In fact, the player who doesn't really understand the strategy of doubling down and of splitting pairs (and many players don't) is giving up some important equalizers. Such players are destined to lose, for they forfeit one of the critical advantages a player has in playing Black Jack which are precious few. The major advantage of doubling is you are allowed to double your bet at a time when the Dealer does not have a favorable card showing and is, therefore, by all probabilities the most vulnerable.

To my way of thinking, Doubling Down is the premier option for the player. It is also often the least understood and least used strategy. Since you will have a worthwile opportunity to Double Down nearly one hand in every ten, (under Las Vegas rules) you can see how imperative it is for you to master this strategy.

CHART NO. 8

Hard Doubling or Hitting

	DEALER SHOWS									
YOUR TOTAL	2	3	4	5	6	7	8	9	10	ACE
8	H	H	H	H	H	H	H	H	H	H
9	H	D	D	D	D	H	H	H	H	H
10	D	D	D	D	D	D	D	D	H	H
11	D	D	D	D	D	D	D	D	D	H

CHART NO. 9

Soft Doubling or Hit or Stand

	DEALER SHOWS									
YOUR HAND	2	3	4	5	6	7	8	9	10	ACE
A,2	H	H	H	D	D	H	H	H	H	H
A,3	H	H	H	D	D	H	H	H	H	H
A,4	H	H	D	D	D	H	H	H	H	H
A,5	H	H	D	D	D	H	H	H	H	H
A,6	H	D	D	D	D	H	H	H	H	H
A,7	S	D	D	D	D	S	S	H	H	H
A,8	S	S	S	S	S	S	S	S	S	S
A,9	S	S	S	S	S	S	S	S	S	S

Under the liberal rules as played in Las Vegas and Atlantic City, you are allowed to double down on *any* two cards. Other casinos are not so liberal. Some allow doubling only on the count of 11. Some, on 10 and 11. Still others, on 9, 10 and 11. Check the rules of the casino before you begin playing. You give up a great deal when you are limited in any way.

I would hope that as the competition between casinos grows, more will convert to liberal doubling. This is certainly one of the reasons for the popularity of Las Vegas casinos. As players become more knowledgeable they will stay away from the more stringent of these casinos. I do.

The master strategy charts for doubling down are shown on the left. Study them well. Train yourself to think doubling. As in pair splitting, this is your golden opportunity for doubling your bet, and for doing so when the Dealer has an unfavorable card showing. You should master the hard doubling down strategy first. About 8.0% of your hands will result in a total of 9, 10, or 11 on which you should double down. About 1.6% of your hands will result in soft totals on which you should double down.

THE MATHEMATICS OF DOUBLING DOWN

Should the basic strategy have you doubling down on a total of 8? The illustrated chart for the hard count of 8 which follows says "NO". For example, if you hold your 8 total against a dealer 5 and simply hit it until you get 12 or more you will win 54% and lose 46% for an 8% advantage. If you double down you will win only 51% and lose 49% for a 2% advantage. However, this 2% must be doubled before comparison since you would be betting twice as much when you double. For every $100 that you bet in this situation you will average an $8 gain by hitting. If you double down you will average 2% of $200 for a $4 gain. Thus hitting wins $4 more, or in other words, is favored by 4% over doubling down. That's what the "H + 4" in the chart means. This is computed by $(54 - 46) - 2x (51 - 49)$ or $8 - 4 = 4$.

Doubling down* is often recommended even though it results in winning the hand less frequently than hitting! Consider a total of 9 versus a dealer 5. If you hit until you get 12 or more you will win 59% of the hands, but if you double you will win only 57% of the hands. That's because if you hit your 9 with a deuce you can hit once again, whereas if you double and get a deuce you are forced to stand and hope the dealer busts. Now consider the mathematics: If you hit you gain 59 − 41 or $18 per $100. If you double you gain 2 x (57 − 43) or $28 or an additional $10 for every $100 initially bet! True, you have to risk twice as much money, but the bottom line is more chips being transferred from the dealer's rack to your side of the table, on average.

Let's take one further example. Consider holding an ace, seven or soft count of 18 against a dealer's 3. If you do not double, you would of course, stand, so we will compare these two strategies. If you stand you win 58% and if you double you would win only 54%. Now this time if you make the type of calculation we showed before you would get a 16% gain for doubling and also a 16% gain for standing, yet the illustrated chart is marked "D + 3". That's because my figures are computed from data accurate to 4 decimal places and rounded off to the nearest percent in most cases. This round off can result in some figures which may look slightly off. In this case doubling wins slightly less than 54.5% so it was rounded down to 54.

---

* Remember, you receive only one card when doubling down.

Standing wins 57.6% so it was rounded up to 58%. Therefore, the more detailed calculation shows doubling wins about 18% of the initial amount of money bet compared to 15.2% for standing or an advantage in favor of doubling of about 2.8% which was rounded to 3%. (If you should find any discrepancies in the chart that seem to exceed 4%, then its probably a typographical error and I would appreciate your telling the publisher about it. Small differences are usually due to similar round off situations.)

In Chapter 2 we talked about the way to play hard counts of 12 to 17. There our objective was to optimize our play *by losing less.* In the case of doubling down we choose to do so only when we have a winning hand and only when it increases our winnings. Clearly, *doubling down is a strategy for winning by winning more.* Let's look now at each of the possibilities. for doing so.

DOUBLING DOWN IN THE SINGLE DECK GAME

The correct basic strategy for doubling in the single deck game is similar to the four deck game with the following important additions — you also double down when holding:

> A total of 11 versus dealer's ace.
>
> A total of 9 versus dealer's two.
>
> A holding of 5,3 versus dealer's 5 or 6.
>
> A holding of A,2 or A,3 versus dealer's 4.
>
> A holding of A,6 versus dealer's two.
>
> A holding of A,8 versus dealer's six.

Also, if you are not allowed to double down after splitting pairs you would double down on a holding of 4,4 versus a dealer's 5 or 6.

DEALER SHOWS

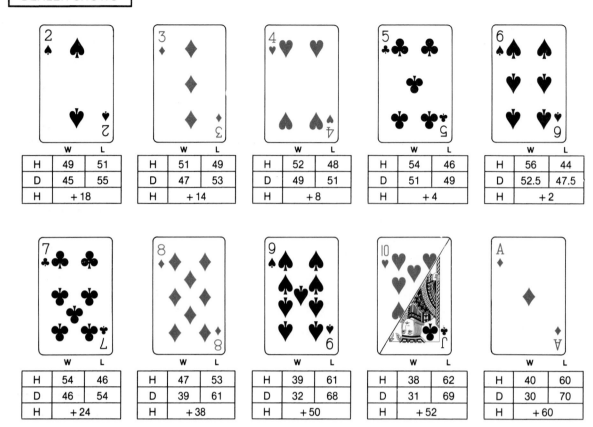

	W	L
H	49	51
D	45	55
H	+18	

	W	L
H	51	49
D	47	53
H	+14	

	W	L
H	52	48
D	49	51
H	+8	

	W	L
H	54	46
D	51	49
H	+4	

	W	L
H	56	44
D	52.5	47.5
H	+2	

	W	L
H	54	46
D	46	54
H	+24	

	W	L
H	47	53
D	39	61
H	+38	

	W	L
H	39	61
D	32	68
H	+50	

	W	L
H	38	62
D	31	69
H	+52	

	W	L
H	40	60
D	30	70
H	+60	

YOUR CARDS

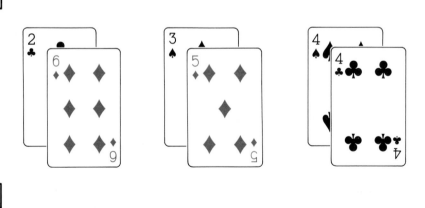

RECAP

	2	3	4	5	6	7	8	9	10	A
8	H	H	H	H	H	H	H	H	H	H
	+18	+14	+8	+4	+2	+24	+38	+50	+52	+60

COMMENTS

This page demonstrates the basic strategy rule that you should always hit a hard count of 8 against any dealer up card rather than doubling down. Of course, you would also hit hard counts of 5, 6, or 7 as well.

DEALER SHOWS

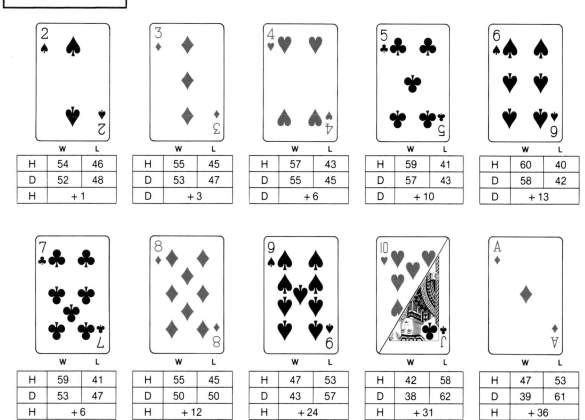

	W	L
H	54	46
D	52	48
H	+1	

	W	L
H	55	45
D	53	47
D	+3	

	W	L
H	57	43
D	55	45
D	+6	

	W	L
H	59	41
D	57	43
D	+10	

	W	L
H	60	40
D	58	42
D	+13	

	W	L
H	59	41
D	53	47
H	+6	

	W	L
H	55	45
D	50	50
H	+12	

	W	L
H	47	53
D	43	57
H	+24	

	W	L
H	42	58
D	38	62
H	+31	

	W	L
H	47	53
D	39	61
H	+36	

YOUR CARDS

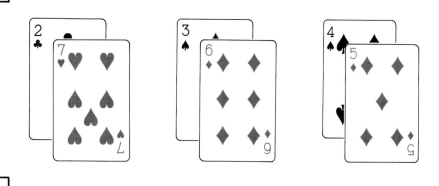

RECAP

	2	3	4	5	6	7	8	9	10	A
9	H	D	D	D	D	H	H	H	H	H
	+1	+3	+6	+10	+13	+6	+12	+24	+31	+36

COMMENTS

With a hard count of 9 you double against a dealer's up card of 3, 4, 5, or 6.

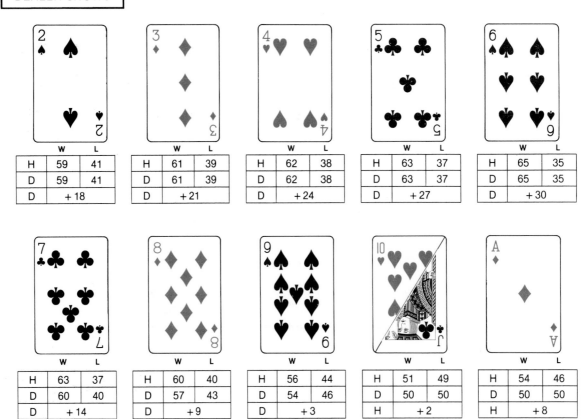

	W	L
H	59	41
D	59	41
D	+18	

	W	L
H	61	39
D	61	39
D	+21	

	W	L
H	62	38
D	62	38
D	+24	

	W	L
H	63	37
D	63	37
D	+27	

	W	L
H	65	35
D	65	35
D	+30	

	W	L
H	63	37
D	60	40
D	+14	

	W	L
H	60	40
D	57	43
D	+9	

	W	L
H	56	44
D	54	46
D	+3	

	W	L
H	51	49
D	50	50
H	+2	

	W	L
H	54	46
D	50	50
H	+8	

YOUR CARDS

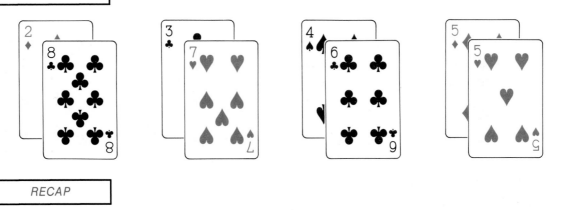

RECAP

	2	3	4	5	6	7	8	9	10	A
10	D	D	D	D	D	D	D	D	H	H
	+18	+21	+24	+27	+30	+14	+9	+3	+2	+8

COMMENTS

With a hard count of 10 you double except when the dealer shows a ten or ace. This is an extremely important strategy.

13 / BASIC STRATEGY FOR THE HARD COUNT OF   11

DEALER SHOWS

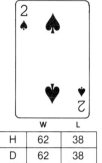

	W	L
H	62	38
D	62	38
D	+24	

	W	L
H	63	37
D	63	37
D	+26	

	W	L
H	65	35
D	65	35
D	+29	

	W	L
H	66	34
D	66	34
D	+32	

	W	L
H	67	33
D	67	33
D	+34	

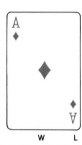

	W	L
H	65	35
D	62	38
D	+17	

	W	L
H	61	39
D	59	41
D	+12	

	W	L
H	58	42
D	56	44
D	+7	

	W	L
H	56	44
D	54	45
D	+6	

	W	L
H	57	43
D	53	47
H	+2	

YOUR CARDS

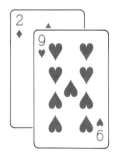
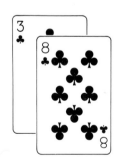
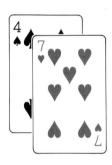
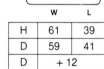

RECAP

	2	3	4	5	6	7	8	9	10	A
	D	D	D	D	D	D	D	D	D	H
11	+24	+26	+29	+32	+34	+17	+12	+7	+6	+2

COMMENTS

With a hard count of 11 you double except when the dealer shows an ace. This is an extremely important strategy.

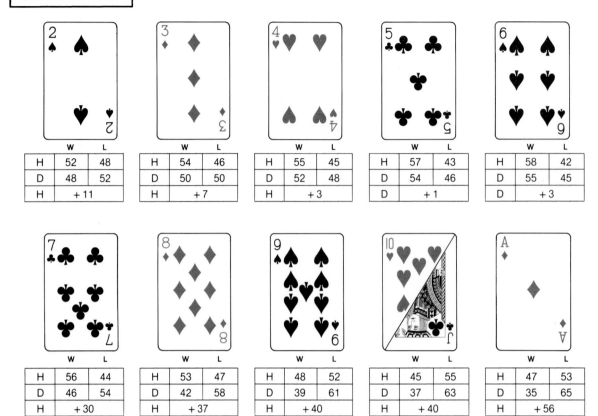

DEALER SHOWS

	W	L
H	52	48
D	48	52
H	+11	

	W	L
H	54	46
D	50	50
H	+7	

	W	L
H	55	45
D	52	48
H	+3	

	W	L
H	57	43
D	54	46
D	+1	

	W	L
H	58	42
D	55	45
D	+3	

	W	L
H	56	44
D	46	54
H	+30	

	W	L
H	53	47
D	42	58
H	+37	

	W	L
H	48	52
D	39	61
H	+40	

	W	L
H	45	55
D	37	63
H	+40	

	W	L
H	47	53
D	35	65
H	+56	

YOUR CARDS

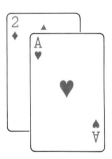

RECAP

	2	3	4	5	6	7	8	9	10	A
	H	H	H	D	D	H	H	H	H	H
A,2	+11	+7	+3	+1	+3	+30	+37	+40	+40	+56

COMMENTS

Double down with A, 2 against a dealer 5 or 6 for a small gain.

DEALER SHOWS

	W	L
H	51	49
D	48	52
H	+9	

	W	L
H	53	47
D	50	50
H	+5	

	W	L
H	54	46
D	52	48
H	+1	

	W	L
H	56	44
D	54	46
D	+3	

	W	L
H	57	43
D	55	45
D	+5	

	W	L
H	54	46
D	45	55
H	+26	

	W	L
H	51	49
D	42	58
H	+32	

	W	L
H	46	54
D	39	61
H	+37	

	W	L
H	43	57
D	37	63
H	+37	

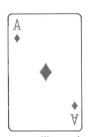

	W	L
H	45	55
D	35	65
H	+52	

YOUR CARDS

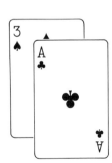

RECAP

	2	3	4	5	6	7	8	9	10	A
	H	H	H	D	D	H	H	H	H	H
A,3	+9	+5	+1	+3	+5	+26	+32	+37	+37	+52

COMMENTS

Double down with A, 3 against a dealer 5 or 6 for a small gain.

DEALER SHOWS

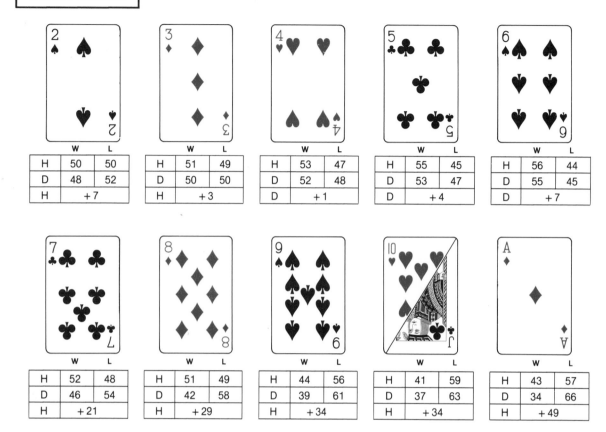

	W	L
H	50	50
D	48	52
H	+7	

	W	L
H	51	49
D	50	50
H	+3	

	W	L
H	53	47
D	52	48
D	+1	

	W	L
H	55	45
D	53	47
D	+4	

	W	L
H	56	44
D	55	45
D	+7	

	W	L
H	52	48
D	46	54
H	+21	

	W	L
H	51	49
D	42	58
H	+29	

	W	L
H	44	56
D	39	61
H	+34	

	W	L
H	41	59
D	37	63
H	+34	

	W	L
H	43	57
D	34	66
H	+49	

YOUR CARDS

RECAP

	2	3	4	5	6	7	8	9	10	A
A,4	H	H	D	D	D	H	H	H	H	H
	+7	+3	+1	+4	+7	+21	+29	+34	+34	+49

COMMENTS

Double down with A, 4 against a dealer 4, 5, or 6 for a small gain.

46

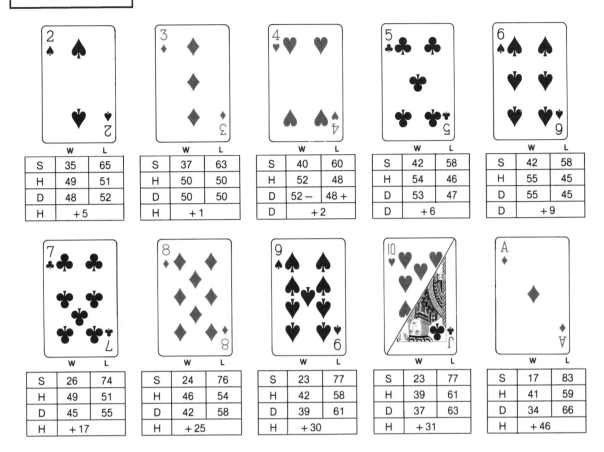

DEALER SHOWS

2♠		
	W	L
S	35	65
H	49	51
D	48	52
H	+5	

3♦		
	W	L
S	37	63
H	50	50
D	50	50
H	+1	

4♥		
	W	L
S	40	60
H	52	48
D	52 −	48 +
D	+2	

5♣		
	W	L
S	42	58
H	54	46
D	53	47
D	+6	

6♠		
	W	L
S	42	58
H	55	45
D	55	45
D	+9	

7♣		
	W	L
S	26	74
H	49	51
D	45	55
H	+17	

8♦		
	W	L
S	24	76
H	46	54
D	42	58
H	+25	

9♠		
	W	L
S	23	77
H	42	58
D	39	61
H	+30	

10♥/J		
	W	L
S	23	77
H	39	61
D	37	63
H	+31	

A♦		
	W	L
S	17	83
H	41	59
D	34	66
H	+46	

YOUR CARDS

RECAP

	2	3	4	5	6	7	8	9	10	A,5
A,5	H	H	D	D	D	H	H	H	H	H
	+5	+1	+2	+6	+9	+17	+25	+30	+31	+46

COMMENTS

Double down with A,5 against a dealer 4, 5, or 6. Notice that you should never stand with a soft total of 16. As you can see from the above data, standing on soft 16 would be an inferior strategy.

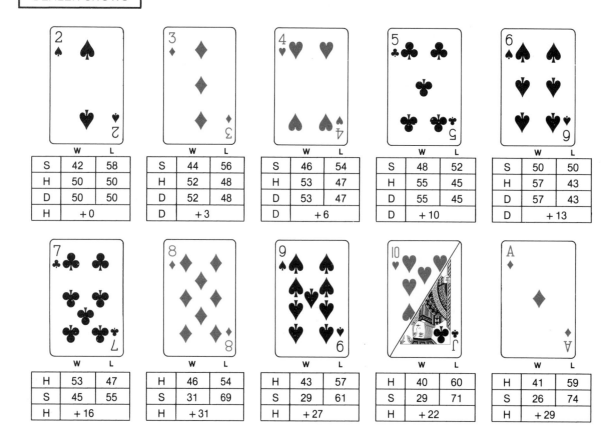

DEALER SHOWS

2♠

	W	L
S	42	58
H	50	50
D	50	50
H	+0	

3♦

	W	L
S	44	56
H	52	48
D	52	48
D	+3	

4♥

	W	L
S	46	54
H	53	47
D	53	47
D	+6	

5♣

	W	L
S	48	52
H	55	45
D	55	45
D	+10	

6♠

	W	L
S	50	50
H	57	43
D	57	43
D	+13	

7♣

	W	L
H	53	47
S	45	55
H	+16	

8♦

	W	L
H	46	54
S	31	69
H	+31	

9♠

	W	L
H	43	57
S	29	61
H	+27	

10♥ / J♣

	W	L
H	40	60
S	29	71
H	+22	

A♦

	W	L
H	41	59
S	26	74
H	+29	

YOUR CARDS

RECAP

A,6	2	3	4	5	6	7	8	9	10	A,6
	H	D	D	D	D	H	H	H	H	H
	+0	+3	+6	+10	+13	+16	+31	+27	+22	+29

COMMENTS

Double down with A,6 against a dealer 3, 4, 5, or 6 for a small to moderate gain. Notice that standing with soft 17 is never recommended.

	W	L
D	53	47
S	56	44
S	+0	

	W	L
D	54	46
S	58	42
D	+3	

	W	L
D	56	44
S	59	41
D	+7	

	W	L
D	58	42
S	60	40
D	+10	

	W	L
D	60	40
S	64	36
D	+11	

    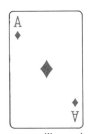

	W	L
H	59	41
S	70	30
S	+23	

	W	L
H	52	48
S	55	45
S	+7	

	W	L
H	45	55
S	41	59
H	+8	

	W	L
H	43	57
S	41	59
H	+4	

	W	L
H	45	55
S	45	55
H	+0.4	

	2	3	4	5	6	7	8	9	10	A
	S	D	D	D	D	S	S	H	H	H
A,7	+0	+3	+7	+10	+11	+23	+7	+8	+4	+0.4

Double down with A, 7 against a dealer 3, 4, 5, 6 for a small to moderate gain. Stand against a dealer 2, 7, or 8. Hit against a dealer 9, 10, or Ace - if hand becomes hard 12 to 16 hit further until at least 17.

DEALER SHOWS

	W	L
D	59	41
S	82	18
S	+28	

	W	L
D	58	42
S	70	30
S	+10	

	W	L
D	59	41
S	71	29
S	+7	

	W	L
D	60	40
S	72	28
S	+3	

	W	L
D	62	38
S	75	25
S	+1	

	W	L
D	58	42
S	81	19
S	+29	

	W	L
D	55	45
S	80	20
S	+40	

	W	L
H	50	50
S	64	36
S	+28	

	W	L
H	46	54
S	53	47
S	+15	

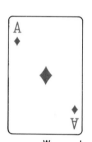

	W	L
H	50	50
S	64	36
S	+29	

YOUR CARDS

RECAP

	2	3	4	5	6	7	8	9	10	A
A,8	S	S	S	S	S	S	S	S	S	S
	+28	+10	+7	+3	+1	+29	+40	+28	+15	+29

COMMENTS

On a total of soft 19 always stand against any dealer up card. Obviously, you would also stand on a soft 20 so we have omitted the detailed chart for this.

50

SPLITTING PAIRS

Almost everyone at one time or another has heard, you "always split Aces and eights." True enough, but why? What about sevens or fours or nines?

Remember our objective. It is to play winning Blackjack. I know of no other way to do it than to play each and every hand the very best way, particularly when the odds are in your favor. Some of those hands will be pairs. You can expect that 144 hands of every 1000 will be pairs, but only 21 of these hands should be split.

When splitting pairs, you are electing to play each card as a separate hand. You will thus have two bets going. You do this, of course, whenever the Dealer's card is in your favor. One additional advantage is that the most liberal rules permit you to split again or even to double down after getting your second card. Under these circumstances, it is conceivable you could be playing three or four hands as a result of splitting that first pair. Don't let such opportunities go by. They are the stuff big winnings are made from.

Chart 21, "SPLITTING PAIRS" illustrates the master strategy for splitting or not splitting.

CHART NO. 21

SPLITTING PAIRS

DEALER SHOWS

YOU HAVE	2	3	4	5	6	7	8	9	10	ACE
A,A	SP	SP	SP	SP	SP	SP	SP	SP	SP	SP
2,2	H	H	SP	SP	SP	SP	H	H	H	H
3,3	H	H	SP	SP	SP	SP	H	H	H	H
4,4	H	H	H	H	H	H	H	H	H	H
6,6	H	SP	SP	SP	SP	H	H	H	H	H
7,7	SP	SP	SP	SP	SP	SP	H	H	H	H
8,8	SP	SP	SP	SP	SP	SP	SP	SP	SP	SP
9,9	SP	SP	SP	SP	SP	S	SP	SP	S	S
10,10	S	S	S	S	S	S	S	S	S	S

The above chart assumes you are not allowed to double down after splitting. Recommendations for splitting pairs when rules permit doubling down after split are to be found on the next page.

Note: Never split 5,5.

The detailed charts and recommendations beginning on Page 56 are to be used in those casinos which do not allow doubling down after pair splitting. Chart for splitting in singledeck play appears on Page 65.

CHART NO. 22

SPLITTING PAIRS

When player is allowed to double after splitting

YOU HAVE	DEALER SHOWS									
	2	3	4	5	6	7	8	9	10	ACE
A,A	SP	SP	SP	SP	SP	SP	SP	SP	SP	SP
2,2	SP	SP	SP	SP	SP	SP	H	H	H	H
3,3	SP	SP	SP	SP	SP	SP	H	H	H	H
4,4	H	H	H	SP	SP	H	H	H	H	H
6,6	SP	SP	SP	SP	SP	H	H	H	H	H
7,7	SP	SP	SP	SP	SP	SP	H	H	H	H
8,8	SP	SP	SP	SP	SP	SP	SP	SP	SP	SP
9,9	SP	SP	SP	SP	SP	S	SP	SP	S	S
10,10	S	S	S	S	S	S	S	S	S	S

In this case the liberal rule of allowing doubling down after pair splitting increases the situations where splitting is recommended. By comparing the above chart to the previous chart you can determine that the additional situations are as follows:

    Split 2,2 or 3,3 when dealer shows a 2 or 3.
    Split 4,4 when dealer shows a 5 or 6.
    Split 6,6 when dealer shows a 2.

With these additions you will be splitting approximately 23 hands out of every 1000 hands played.

THE MATHEMATICS OF PAIR SPLITTING

When you split a pair you of course have to bet more. This strategy is recommended when the result, on average, fulfills either of the following two situations:

1) You expect to win more.
2) You expect to lose less.

SPLITTING TO WIN MORE

Consider a holding of 9,9. This is a fairly good hand, especially if the dealer is showing a small card. Suppose the dealer has a 3 showing. If you stand, you win 57%, lose 43% of the time for an average gain of 14%. If you split you will only win about 55% of the hands and lose 45%. Now 2*X (55% − 45%) = 20% which is 6% better than standing. In other words, for every $100 bet on a holding of a pair of 9's versus a dealer 3, you will, on average, gain $6 more by splitting rather than standing.

SPLITTING TO LOSE LESS

Consider a holding of 9, 9 versus a dealer 9. In this case, if you stand on your 18 total, you have a likely loser to the dealer's most probable total of 19. You would win only 40.7% and lose 59.3% of the time for an 18.6% loss of the money wagered. If you split the 9's your most likely total will be 19 which would tie a dealer 19. On average you will win 47.4% and lose 52.6% if you split, for a net loss of 2*X5.2%, or 10.4%. This is clearly better than losing 18.6%. So here we split to lose about $8 less per $100 bet.

---

*2, because you are now betting both of your nines.

54

CHART NO. 32

SPLITTING PAIRS IN THE SINGLE DECK GAME

A. Doubling down after pair-splitting is not allowed.

DEALER SHOWS

YOU HAVE	2	3	4	5	6	7	8	9	10	ACE
A,A	SP	SP	SP	SP	SP	SP	SP	SP	SP	SP
2,2	H	SP	SP	SP	SP	SP	H	H	H	H
3,3	H	H	SP	SP	SP	SP	H	H	H	H
4,4	H	H	H	D	D	H	H	H	H	H
6,6	SP	SP	SP	SP	SP	H	H	H	H	H
7,7	SP	SP	SP	SP	SP	SP	H	H	S	H
8,8	SP	SP	SP	SP	SP	SP	SP	SP	SP	SP
9,9	SP	SP	SP	SP	SP	S	SP	SP	S	S
10,10	S	S	S	S	S	S	S	S	S	S

CHART NO. 33

B. Doubling down after pair-splitting is allowed.

DEALER SHOWS

YOU HAVE	2	3	4	5	6	7	8	9	10	ACE
A,A	SP	SP	SP	SP	SP	SP	SP	SP	SP	SP
2,2	SP	SP	SP	SP	SP	SP	H	H	H	H
3,3	SP	SP	SP	SP	SP	SP	H	H	H	H
4,4	H	H	SP	SP	SP	H	H	H	H	H
6,6	SP	SP	SP	SP	SP	SP	H	H	H	H
7,7	SP	SP	SP	SP	SP	SP	SP	H	S	H
8,8	SP	SP	SP	SP	SP	SP	SP	SP	SP	SP
9,9	SP	SP	SP	SP	SP	S	SP	SP	S	S
10,10	S	S	S	S	S	S	S	S	S	S

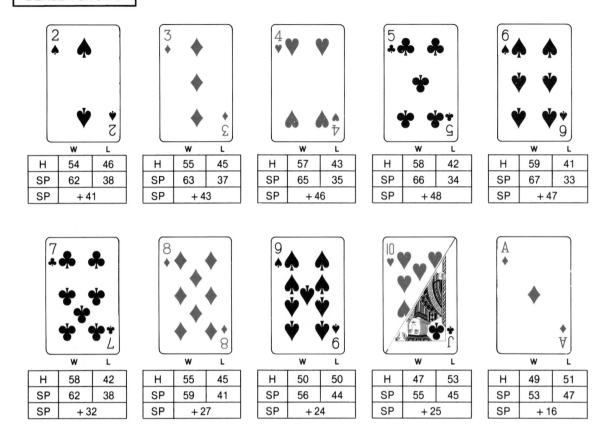

	W	L
H	54	46
SP	62	38
SP	+41	

	W	L
H	55	45
SP	63	37
SP	+43	

	W	L
H	57	43
SP	65	35
SP	+46	

	W	L
H	58	42
SP	66	34
SP	+48	

	W	L
H	59	41
SP	67	33
SP	+47	

	W	L
H	58	42
SP	62	38
SP	+32	

	W	L
H	55	45
SP	59	41
SP	+27	

	W	L
H	50	50
SP	56	44
SP	+24	

	W	L
H	47	53
SP	55	45
SP	+25	

	W	L
H	49	51
SP	53	47
SP	+16	

YOUR CARDS

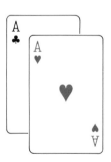

RECAP

	2	3	4	5	6	7	8	9	10	A
A,A	SP	SP	SP	SP	SP	SP	SP	SP	SP	SP
	+41	+43	+46	+48	+47	+32	+27	+24	+25	+16

COMMENTS

An extremely important strategy! Always split aces. On average it results in significant gains.

	W	L
H	44	56
SP	46	54
H	+3	

	W	L
H	46	54
SP	48	52
H	+1	

	W	L
H	48	52
SP	49	51
SP	+1	

	W	L
H	50	50
SP	51	49
SP	+5	

	W	L
H	51	49
SP	52	48
SP	+7	

	W	L
H	46	54
SP	49	51
SP	+3	

	W	L
H	42	58
SP	45	55
H	+5	

	W	L
H	38	62
SP	40	60
H	+15	

	W	L
H	36	64
SP	38	62
H	+19	

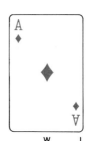

	W	L
H	37	63
SP	40	60
H	+16	

YOUR CARDS

RECAP

	2	3	4	5	6	7	8	9	10	A
2,2	H	H	SP	SP	SP	SP	H	H	H	H
	+3	+1	+1	+5	+7	+3	+5	+15	+19	+16

COMMENTS

Split deuces whenever the dealer shows a 4, 5, 6, or 7. Note that against the dealer 4 or 7 you will still win less than 50% of the time, but you will gain through the process of losing less money.

DEALER SHOWS

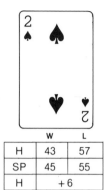

	W	L
H	43	57
SP	45	55
H	+6	

	W	L
H	45	55
SP	47	53
H	+3	

	W	L
H	47	53
SP	49	51
SP	+1	

	W	L
H	49	51
SP	50	50
SP	+4	

	W	L
H	50	50
SP	51	49
SP	+6	

	W	L
H	42	58
SP	47	53
SP	+4	

	W	L
H	39	61
SP	43	57
H	+4	

	W	L
H	35	65
SP	39	61
H	+13	

	W	L
H	33	67
SP	37	63
H	+18	

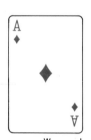

	W	L
H	34	66
SP	38	62
H	+15	

YOUR CARDS

RECAP

	2	3	4	5	6	7	8	9	10	A
3,3	H	H	SP	SP	SP	SP	H	H	H	H
	+6	+3	+1	+4	+6	+4	+4	+13	+18	+15

COMMENTS

Split three's against a dealer 4, 5, 6 or 7. Note that against the dealer 4 or 7 you will still win less than 50% of the time, but you will gain through the process of losing less.

DEALER SHOWS

	W	L
H	49	51
SP	44	56
H	+21	

	W	L
H	51	49
SP	46	54
H	+17	

	W	L
H	53	47
SP	48	52
H	+14	

	W	L
H	54	46
SP	50	50
H	+10	

	W	L
H	56	44
SP	51	49
H	+10	

	W	L
H	54	46
SP	45	55
H	+28	

	W	L
H	47	53
SP	42	58
H	+26	

	W	L
H	39	61
SP	38	62
H	+37	

	W	L
H	38	62
SP	36	64
H	+33	

	W	L
H	46	54
SP	37	63
H	+31	

YOUR CARDS

RECAP

	2	3	4	5	6	7	8	9	10	A
	H	H	H	H	H	H	H	H	H	H
4,4	+21	+17	+14	+10	+10	+28	+26	+37	+33	+31

COMMENTS

Always hit 4's when you are not allowed to double down after splitting. For situations where splitting 4's is recommended see Page 53.

DEALER SHOWS

	W	L
H	37	63
SP	43	57
H	+2	

	W	L
H	38	62
SP	45	55
SP	+3	

	W	L
S	40	60
SP	47	53
SP	+7	

	W	L
S	42	58
SP	49	51
SP	+10	

	W	L
S	42	58
SP	49	51
SP	+13	

	W	L
H	39	61
SP	43	57
H	+7	

	W	L
H	36	64
SP	39	61
H	+15	

	W	L
H	32	68
SP	35	65
H	+23	

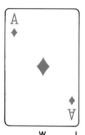

	W	L
H	31	69
SP	33	67
H	+29	

	W	L
H	32	68
SP	35	65
H	+25	

YOUR CARDS

RECAP

	2	3	4	5	6	7	8	9	10	A
6,6	H	SP	SP	SP	SP	H	H	H	H	H
	+2	+3	+7	+10	+13	+7	+15	+23	+29	+25

COMMENTS

An undesirable hand! However, if the dealer shows a 3, 4, 5, or 6 you can improve your prospects somewhat by splitting, resulting, on average, in losing less.

DEALER SHOWS·

	W	L
S	36	64
SP	45	55
SP	+8	

	W	L
S	38	62
SP	46	54
SP	+10	

	W	L
S	40	60
SP	48	52
SP	+13	

	W	L
S	42	58
SP	50	50
SP	+16	

	W	L
S	42	58
SP	52	48
SP	+22	

   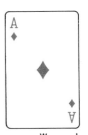 

	W	L
H	33	67
SP	47	53
SP	+20	

	W	L
H	31	69
SP	39	61
H	+4	

	W	L
H	28	72
SP	36	64
H	+13	

	W	L
H	26	74
SP	34	66
H	+16	

	W	L
H	27	73
SP	34	66
H	+17	

YOUR CARDS

RECAP

	2	3	4	5	6	7	8	9	10	A
	SP	SP	SP	SP	SP	SP	H	H	H	H
7,7	+8	+10	+13	+16	+22	+20	+4	+13	+16	+17

COMMENTS

An undesirable hand! However, against a dealer 2 through 7 split your pair of 7's to improve your prospects.

DEALER SHOWS

 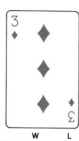   

	W	L
S	36	64
SP	49	51
SP	+ 25	

	W	L
S	38	62
SP	51	49
SP	+ 27	

	W	L
S	39	61
SP	52	48
SP	+ 30	

	W	L
S	42	58
SP	54	46
SP	+ 32	

	W	L
S	42	58
SP	56	44
SP	+ 39	

	W	L
H	30	70
SP	54	46
SP	+ 58	

	W	L
H	27	73
SP	47	53
SP	+ 34	

	W	L
H	25	75
SP	40	60
SP	+ 9	

	W	L
H	23	77
SP	38	62
SP	+ 5	

	W	L
H	24	76
SP	40	60
SP	+ 12	

YOUR CARDS

RECAP

	2	3	4	5	6	7	8	9	10	A
8,8	SP	SP	SP	SP	SP	SP	SP	SP	SP	SP
	+ 25	+ 27	+ 30	+ 32	+ 39	+ 58	+ 34	+ 9	+ 5	+ 12

COMMENTS

A pair of 8's is a bad hand. Split the pair to get a fair chance at some winning hands. Against a dealer 3 to 7 you will usually convert a loser to winners. Against a dealer 2, 8, 9, 10 or Ace you will usually still lose, but you will lose less.

	W	L
S	56	44
SP	54	46
SP	+2	

	W	L
S	57	43
SP	55	45
SP	+6	

	W	L
S	59	41
SP	57	43
SP	+9	

	W	L
S	60	40
SP	58	42
SP	+13	

	W	L
S	64	36
SP	60	40
SP	+11	

	W	L
S	70	30
SP	59	41
S	+6	

	W	L
S	55	45
SP	55	45
SP	+10	

	W	L
S	41	59
SP	47	53
SP	+8	

	W	L
S	42	58
SP	43	57
S	+13	

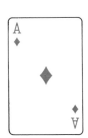

	W	L
S	46	54
SP	47	53
S	+4	

YOUR CARDS

RECAP

	2	3	4	5	6	7	8	9	10	A
9,9	SP	SP	SP	SP	SP	S	SP	SP	S	S
	+2	+6	+9	+13	+11	+6	+10	+8	+13	+4

COMMENTS

Stand against a dealer Ace, ten, or 7. Otherwise, split. If the dealer shows a 7 your 18 total will already beat the dealer's most likely total of 17 so you don't split.

	W	L
S	82	18
SP	59	41
S	+28	

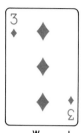

	W	L
S	82	18
SP	60	40
S	+24	

	W	L
S	83	17
SP	61	39
S	+20	

	W	L
S	84	16
SP	63	37
S	+16	

	W	L
S	85	15
SP	64	36
S	+13	

	W	L
S	89	11
SP	62	38
S	+27	

	W	L
S	89	11
SP	60	40
S	+41	

	W	L
S	88	12
SP	55	45
S	+54	

	W	L
S	78	22
SP	51	49
S	+51	

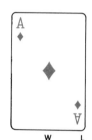

	W	L
S	82	18
SP	54	46
S	+51	

YOUR CARDS

RECAP

	2	3	4	5	6	7	8	9	10	A
10,10	S	S	S	S	S	S	S	S	S	S
	+28	+24	+20	+16	+13	+27	+41	+54	+51	+51

COMMENTS

Never split tens. You have too good a hand. Even against a dealer 6 or 5 you will be 13% to 16% better off standing than splitting.

The recommendations shown in the preceding individual charts for splitting, as well as those charts for doubling down, are summarized on the basic strategy chart on page 24.

5

SURRENDER AND INSURANCE

SURRENDER

There are several forms of the surrender rule in existence. Most casinos do not offer it at all. Where it is offered it can be most useful for the knowledgeable player. Surrender suggests giving up something and so we have used a "G" in the earlier diagrams where it is applicable.

The surrender rule seems to have been first introduced in 1958 by the Continental Casino in Manila. It then spread to nearly all the casinos in the Far East. The usual rule in the Far Eastern casinos is the player may throw in any hand containing any number of cards whose total value does not exceed 21 providing the dealer does not show an ace, and give up half his bet for doing so. Further, if the dealer has a ten up, surrender can be employed only after the dealer has looked at his hole card and finds he does not have a blackjack.

In the Las Vegas casinos having the surrender option, only the player's two card original hand can be surrendered and in case the dealer has an ace or ten showing, only after the dealer has examined his hole card and ascertained he does not have a blackjack. This is sometimes described as "late surrender" to distinguish it from "early surrender" to be described later.

It may go against the grain of some players to give up half their wager, but if you have a hand where you will lose, on average, more than 50% of the wager, then surrender is a worthwhile strategy to employ. Surrender is only recommended on hands that will lose over 75% of the time.

Consider, for example, the situation where you hold a hard count of 16 against a dealer 10. With best play, which is to hit this hand once, you win 23.4% of the hands and lose 76.6% for a loss of $53.20, on average, for every $100 wagered. If you surrender you would lose exactly $50.00 instead, which is 3.2% better. This is shown as "G + 3" in the illustrated chart for this situation shown earlier. Clearly, surrender, when properly employed is a strategy for winning by *losing less*.

The basic strategy of surrender indicates that you should surrender only the following hands:

(10,6) versus a dealer 9,10, or Ace
(9,7) versus a dealer 9,10 or Ace
(10,5) versus a dealer 10
(9,6) versus a dealer 10

The use of this strategy will increase your overall average win rate by .065%. The surrender of (10,6) and (9,7) against a dealer 9 is just barely worthwhile. If you omit these two plays, but incorporate the other good surrenders you will still gain .064%.

For a single deck game the correct basic strategy indicates that only the following hands should be surrendered:

(10,6) versus a dealer 10 or Ace

(9,7) versus a dealer 10

(10,5) versus a dealer 10

(9,6) versus a dealer 10

(7,7) versus a dealer 10

In the single deck game the Las Vegas late surrender rule is only worth .022% overall to the basic strategy player.

EARLY SURRENDER

In 1978 Resorts International opened a casino in Atlantic City, New Jersey. Their Blackjack games have the following features:

1. The dealer takes a hole card but does not look at it until after the players have completed their hands. If the player should split a pair or double down and the dealer gets a blackjack the player loses only the original bet.

2. Player may surrender any first two cards, even if the dealer shows a ten or Ace.

3. Player may double down on any two card holding. Player may double down after splitting a pair.

4. Any pair may be split but resplitting is not allowed.

5. Dealer stands on all 17's.

6. Four or more decks are used.

7. Insurance is offered.

Note especially items 1 and 2. The player can actually surrender against a potential blackjack! When the dealer has an ace up the dealer will get a blackjack 4/13's of the time. To surrender against a potential dealer black-jack before the dealer has determined his hole card is often called "early surrender," or "no-hole card surrender." The correct basic strategy of surrender for this rule is as follows:

1) Versus a dealer ace surrender all hard counts of 5 to 7 and 12 to 17.

2) Versus a dealer ten surrender all hard counts of 14 to 16. It should be noted that the hard 14's against a dealer ten are just barely worth surrendering if the aces remaining in the pack are at a normal amount. If the player should happen to note that the aces remaining are somewhat below normal then the hard 14's should not be sur-rendered in this case.

3) As usual, surrender holdings of (10,6) and (9,7) versus a dealer nine.

Employment of this player option in casinos where it is offered is quite im-portant as it will gain the basic strategy player nearly 5/8 of one percent overall (.624%, to be exact!). The percentage gain is far greater in many of the individual hands.

Recently, a second casino, the Boardwalk Regency, opened in Atlantic City and more are expected to follow. The New Jersey Gaming Commis-sion establishes the rules and presumably all of these casinos will employ the same rules. The basic strategy player who uses all of the player options properly actually has a small edge of a little over .1% in the Atlantic City four deck games.

Some years ago I occasionally encountered a dealer in Las Vegas who erroneously let me surrender before he looked at his hole card when he had an ace up! Even today, it may be worth a try.

FIVE CARD SURRENDER

In many of the casinos in the Far East a second form of surrender is also often offered: If the player succeeds in getting five cards without going over 21 he may exhibit this result and relinquish his hand receiving back his original wager plus winnings of one-half his original wager. The player in this case is guaranteed a "half win" and gives up the possibility of a "full win." The special basic strategy plays for this rule in combination with late surrender as it is played in the Far Eastern casinos is approximately as follows:

1) Stand on a five card 20 or 21.

2) Surrender a five card 19 unless the dealer shows a 7 or 8.

3) Always surrender a five card holding of 18 or less regardless of the dealer's up card.

4) Hit all 4 card holdings of hard 12 to 14.

5) Hit all 4 card holdings of hard 15 if the dealer shows a 2, 7, 8, 9, 10, or Ace.

6) Hit 4 card holdings of hard 16 if the dealer shows 7, 8, 9, 10 or Ace.

7) Always hit 2 to 4 card holdings of soft 18 or less.

8) Always hit a 4 card holding of soft 19.

9) When doubling down and the dealer shows an 8, 9, or 10 surrender the hand if the three card total is less than 17.

10) Surrender all hard totals of 16 (other than 8,8) consisting of 2 or 3 cards against a dealer 10 or 9.

11) Surrender all hard totals of 15 except (8,7) consisting of 2 or 3 cards against a dealer 10.

12) Do not split 2,2.

There are numerous variations in the rules in the Far Eastern casinos. For exact details refer to Stanford Wong's *Blackjack in Asia*.

INSURANCE

Insurance was briefly mentioned in Chapter 1. Whenever the dealer shows an Ace as his face up card the dealer will in most U.S. casinos ask "Insurance?" You are then given the option of making a separate wager that the dealer has a ten as a hole card. If you make this wager you are usually limited to making an insurance bet of at most half the original bet. After everyone has had an opportunity to make this wager the dealer looks at his hole card. If the dealer has a ten in the hole he shows it and pays off the insurance bets two to one. If the dealer does not have a ten in the hole the insurance bets are lost by the players making them and play continues. The original bet is settled in the usual way regardless of the outcome of the insurance bet.

Suppose, for example, that you are betting $10 on your hand. You do not have a blackjack and the dealer shows an ace. Let's say you decide to take insurance. You place a $5 chip on the semicircular portion of the layout labeled "Insurance pays 2 to 1" in front of your bet. Let's further assume the dealer finds a ten in the hole which he then turns up. You would lose your original $10 bet but would win $10 on the insurance bet for an overall result of no gain or loss. In fact, the dealer, to save time will often simply push your $5 insurance bet back against your original $10 bet, thus paying off your insurance bet with your original wager. If you hadn't taken insurance you would have, of course, lost your $10 bet.

I do not know who invented the insurance wager, but whoever he was it was a stroke of sheer genius that has resulted in significant extra profits for the casinos. Since the insurance bet prevents a loss of money in the event the dealer has a ten underneath his ace, this term seemed appropriate. The notion often arises that the player should insure a good hand, especially a holding of two tens since it would be a shame to lose on such a holding. This kind of player will usually not insure a poor holding. If anything, just the opposite is more apt to be preferable!

First of all, if you make the so-called insurance bet you are *not* insuring anything; you are merely making an additional wager that the dealer has a ten in the hole. Second, the correct basic strategy for insurance is DON'T TAKE INSURANCE! Let us examine the mathematics. If the dealer shows an ace he will have a ten in the hole, on the average, 64 out of 207 hands. Thus, if you take insurance every time the dealer shows an ace you would win twice your insurance wager 64 times and lose your insurance wager the remaining 143 times. Now $(64 \times 2) - 143 = -15$. This means that you would lose $15 for every $207 you bet, a house advantage of $7\frac{1}{4}\%$!

In order for insurance to be worthwhile, over one third of the unseen pack must consist of tens. Thus, if you haven't observed many tens being dealt and if you and the other players have been getting mostly poor hands consisting of small cards, the closer you will be to the point where insurance will be worthwhile. Let's take a simple example. Suppose there are 5 players at the table including yourself. The shoe has just been shuffled and on the first round a total of 18 cards are dealt of which only 2 are tens. On the second round the dealer shows an Ace and all five players get small cards — not a single ten. There are now 62 tens among the remaining 179 cards not yet seen. In this case insurance is advised. You would win 62 times and lose 117 times for a net gain of 62 x 2 - 117 = 7. That is, for every $179 bet you would be $7 ahead in this case for a 3.9% edge. But, do not guess . . . or make insurance bets by hunch! Unless you are carefully observing the cards and really know that over 1/3 of the remaining cards are tens, only then will insurance be worthwhile.

INSURING A BLACKJACK

Some dealers and would-be "smart" players insist you should always take insurance when you hold a blackjack and the dealer shows an ace. This supposition arises from the fact you have a sure win and hence, you ought to take it (?). This is a misconception as I shall show. First let's exhibit the sure win. If the dealer does indeed have a blackjack your blackjack would be a push, but you will win the insurance bet for a gain equal to your original wager. If the dealer does not have a blackjack you will lose the insurance bet (½ wager), but you will win 1½ times your wager for your blackjack for a net gain equal to your original wager. Either way, you win an amount equal to your original wager. When a player insures a blackjack some dealers have been observed to pay off even money before looking at their hole card!

Although you cannot suffer a direct loss when insuring a blackjack the result, on average, is that you will win less! Suppose, in an extreme case, there are absolutely no tens remaining in the pack. If you do not insure, you win 1½ times your bet. If you do insure, you only win what you bet. To insure is to throw away a sure win of an additional half your wager. This would be sheer folly. Suppose, however, the pack contains relatively few tens. Would you insure? No, for to do so, would probably be throwing away the insurance bet.

Suppose you are not particularly observant of the tens and you always insure a blackjack. How much would you be throwing away? Let's say you bet $10 a hand. Out of the other 205 cards, 63 are tens. Therefore, the average results for 205 insurance bets of $5 each are as follows:

You win 2-1 insurance 63 times	+ $	630
You lose your insurance bet 142 times	–	710
You win $15 on your blackjacks 142 times	+	2,130
	TOTAL	$ 2,050

If you did not insure, you would have won a total of $2,130. That is, you would be making $80 less for a total of 205 such hands. Now $80/$2050 = 3.9%, that is, you would be making 3.9% less profit.

If the $80 lost is compared to the total wagered on insurance, which is 205 × $5 = $1,025 the house advantage is 7.8%. This is higher than the previously indicated 7¼% because, if you have a blackjack, the existence of the ten in your hand makes it less likely the dealer has a blackjack, thus increasing the house edge.

This discussion may have seemed a bit long winded, but I want to make sure you understand the important principle — do not make an insurance bet regardless of what you are holding unless you are reasonably certain over one-third of the unseen cards are tens.

Approximate Effect of Common Rules Variations on Player's Advantage When the Basic Strategy Is Used

Rules Variations Based on Comparison to 4 Deck Game	Player's Gain or Loss in Percent
One Deck	+ .5
Two Decks	+ .16
Five Decks	− .03
Six Decks	− .05
Dealer Hits Soft 17	− .2
Double on All Totals After Pair Splitting	+ .14
Forbid Doubling on All Soft Hands	− .1
Forbid Doubling on Hard 9	− .1
Forbid Doubling on Hard 10	− .5
Forbid Doubling on Hard 11	− .8
Allow Doubling on 3 or More Cards	+ .2
Delete Rule of Only One Card to Split Aces	+ .1
Resplit All Pairs Except Aces	+ .1
Resplit All Pairs Including Aces	+ .2
A,J of Spades Always Wins Double	+ .042
Blackjack Always Wins but is Paid Even	− 2.06
Late Surrender (as in Las Vegas)	+ .065
Early Surrender (Atlantic City)	+ .624
Five Card Surrender (Far East)	+ .7*

*According to Stanford Wong. However, this varies with the specific rules variations.

YOU AND THE COMPUTER

The single purpose of this chapter is to support and describe the methods for achieving the results which appear throughout this book. For it is these calculated results which act as justification for all strategy recommendations. I'm aware that most discussions about computers are boring to anyone not in the business. Accordingly, if you wish to take my word as to the accuracy of information, you may not want to spend too much time with this chapter. Some of the historical background however, may prove interesting to you.

Until the mid 1950's, very little if anything in the way of reasonably accurate computations for the game of Black Jack had been done. Various authors had suggested strategies for playing the game, but these strategies were largely guesswork and often quite wrong in comparison with what we know today. In 1953 Roger R. Baldwin, Wilbert E. Cantery, Herbert Maisel and James McDermott were members of the U.S. Army stationed at Aberdeen Proving Ground, Maryland. These men embarked upon the ambitious project of computing the correct way to play Black Jack. Not having access to a high speed electronic computer, they did their work during off duty time on desk calculators. After three years of arduous calculations, they had some answers. They published a technical article "The Optimum Strategy in Blackjack" in the September, 1956 issue of the Journal of the American Statistical Association. In 1957 a New York publisher, M. Barrows & Company, published a more readable and popularized version of their work called *Playing Blackjack to Win*. Now a collectors item, this book has long since been out of print but may be found in some libraries.

The work of the Baldwin group marked the first really serious and significant work on Blackjack to be published. Their results presented a rather close approximation of the correct basic strategy for the game. By "basic strategy" we mean the correct way to play based only upon the player's card holding and the dealer's face up card without remembering or counting any of the cards which have previously been played. The work of the Baldwin group was not highly publicized and little noted at the time. Professor Edward O. Thorp, who at that time was at the Massachusetts Institute of Technology, was one who did notice. Prof. Thorp investigated the Baldwin work carefully and then wrote a generalized program for a high speed computer which would allow any deck composition to be analyzed. Prof. Thorp was the first person to do this; I was the second.

Consider the computer to be your friend. Without its aid it would have been infeasible to accurately develop the complete basic strategy and the various count strategies described later in this book.

Prof. Thorp's work resulted in the book *Beat the Dealer* published in 1962 by the Blaisdell Publishing Co., a division of Random House. A second edition appeared in 1966 and is widely available in both hard and soft cover. Thorp's program was approximate, but it was good enough to develop a winning count strategy. I contacted Dr. Thorp and carried on his work by devising an improved version of his program as well as the first program for computing the exact probabilities for the game. Accordingly, my work has been widely quoted (and sometimes used without acknowledgement) by many other authors.

Baldwin's group believed that the casino had an edge of about .6% with correct basic stategy. Thorp's work improved the strategy and his approximations led him to believe the casino had an edge of about .2%. My work showed that for the single deck, which is about all they played in those days, the *player* actually had a small edge of about .1%. This latter figure was valid only under typical Las Vegas Strip rules, and only under the assumption the player would always play correctly.

THE LAW OF PROBABILITIES-HOW IT WORKS

Let's digress from Blackjack for the moment. Suppose you toss a coin. There are five possibilities:

1) HEADS
2) TAILS
3) STAND ON EDGE
4) LEAN AGAINST SOMETHING
5) DISAPPEAR

If any of the last three occur, toss again or forget it. Let's suppose you are betting on heads. You have a 50% chance of winning any given toss. (We will assume an unbiased coin.) Now suppose you toss the coin 1000 times. Does that mean you will win 500 times? No, of course not. You might win exactly 500 times, but it is more likely the number of wins will be some other number in the range 468 to 532. The law of probabilities simply indicates the long range, average expectation. It should further be realized that a nondefective, randomly tossed coin has no memory. Thus, if heads should come up five times in succession this does not mean that tails are "due"; on the next toss the probability of a tail is still 50%. The essence of these ideas enabled me to "solve" the game of Blackjack with the aid of a computer applying the laws of probability.

RELATIONSHIP OF PROBABILITIES TO BLACKJACK STRATEGY

The tables which follow are for reference only. They are the result of the mathematical equivalents of several billion hands run through a computer. As such, they represent just about everything which can occur when playing Blackjack with four or more decks. They also represent the core of data results obtained from detailed probability calculations.

Please do not let these charts intimidate you. My objectives remain as before, to provide you with as simple a group of rules to follow as possible, and these have already appeared. However, since my work in the field has been alluded to by many others as the foundation for all strategies and systems, I feel compelled to print these findings to be certain you have the accurate Braun tables.

I also suggest that with just a little effort, you will find them easy to comprehend and quite interesting. The two charts which follow represent the average results you can expect from 100,000 hands. Chart No. 34 illustrates how many times you will get each hand. Chart No. 35 pictures your wins and losses while holding each of these hands. In each case the Dealer's open card is shown across the top, while your two card hand or total is shown vertically in the left hand column.

Chart No. 34 is easily computed by applying the law of probabilities on a desk calculator. For example, here's how I computed the probability of holding an A,10 (blackjack) against a dealer's ace. Starting with 4 decks the probability that you will get an ace on your first card is 16/208 since there are 16 aces and 208 cards in all. Then the probability that the dealer gets an ace is 15/207 since 15 aces and 207 cards remain. Finally you yould have 64 chances out of 206 to get a 10. Now (16/208) X (15/207) X (64/206) = .00173. Since I have not listed a holding of 10,A as a separate hand and since this is obviously an equivalent hand we must double the .00173 getting .00346. That is, out of 100,000 hands you will have a blackjack against a dealer ace approximately 346 times. Unless otherwise indicated, all data in this book is for the four deck game.

The computations for chart No. 35 are more complicated. In the case of A,10 versus dealer ace we can readily work this out. Not all of your blackjacks will win against a dealer ace. We must figure out how many will tie and how many will win. Since the dealer may be assumed to be taking his hole card from the remaining 205 cards and since 63 tens remain, the probability he will also have a blackjack is 63/205. Multiplying this fraction by 346 gives 106 which means that on average, of the 346 blackjacks, 106 of them will be tied and 240 of them will win 1½ units. 240 X 1½ = 360, the figure in the table.

CHART NO. 34

How many times you will get each hand
in 100,000 hands

DEALER'S UP CARD

PLAYER'S 2 CARD HAND	A	2	3	4	5	6	7	8	9	10
A,A	38	43	43	43	43	43	43	43	43	173
2,2	43	38	43	43	43	43	43	43	43	173
3,3	43	43	38	43	43	43	43	43	43	173
4,4	43	43	43	38	43	43	43	43	43	173
6,6	43	43	43	43	43	38	43	43	43	173
7,7	43	43	43	43	43	43	38	43	43	173
8,8	43	43	43	43	43	43	43	38	43	173
9,9	43	43	43	43	43	43	43	43	38	173
10,10	727	727	727	727	727	727	727	727	727	2818
A,2	87	87	92	92	92	92	92	92	92	369
A,3	87	92	87	92	92	92	92	92	92	369
A,4	87	92	92	87	92	92	92	92	92	369
A,5	87	92	92	92	87	92	92	92	92	369
A,6	87	92	92	92	92	87	92	92	92	369
A,7	87	92	92	92	92	92	87	92	92	369
A,8	87	92	92	92	92	92	92	87	92	369
A,9	87	92	92	92	92	92	92	92	87	369
A,10	346	369	369	369	369	369	369	369	369	1455
2,3	92	87	87	92	92	92	92	92	92	369
2,4	92	87	92	87	92	92	92	92	92	369
7	185	179	179	179	179	185	185	185	185	739
8	185	179	179	185	179	179	185	185	185	739
9	277	271	271	271	271	271	271	271	271	1108
10	320	315	315	315	309	315	315	315	320	1281
11	369	364	364	364	364	364	364	364	364	1478
12	647	623	641	641	641	647	641	641	641	2563
13	647	647	623	641	641	641	641	641	641	2563
14	554	554	554	531	548	548	554	548	548	2194
15	554	554	554	554	531	548	548	548	548	2194
16	462	462	462	462	462	439	456	462	456	1824
17	462	462	462	462	462	462	439	456	456	1824
18	369	369	369	369	369	369	369	346	369	1455
19	369	369	369	369	369	369	369	369	346	1455

82

CHART NO. 35

How many times you will win or lose
each hand in 100,000 hands

DEALER'S UP CARD

	A	2	3	4	5	6	7	8	9	10	Win	%
A,A	− 8	21	23	25	28	30	21	16	11	18	185	33.2
2,2	− 21	− 4	− 4	− 2	2	4	− 2	− 7	− 10	− 59	− 103	− 18.5
3,3	− 23	− 6	− 5	− 3	1	2	− 5	− 10	− 13	− 67	− 129	− 23.1
4,4	− 19	− 1	1	2	4	6	4	− 3	− 9	− 52	− 67	− 12.0
6,6	− 24	− 10	− 9	− 6	− 2	− 1	− 10	− 12	− 15	− 74	− 163	− 29.2
7,7	− 27	− 9	− 6	− 3	0	3	− 5	− 16	− 19	− 89	− 171	− 30.7
8,8	− 25	− 2	1	4	7	10	8	− 4	− 18	− 91	− 110	− 19.7
9,9	− 16	6	9	11	14	17	17	8	− 4	− 40	22	3.9
10,10	112	463	470	478	488	511	561	574	549	1239	5445	58.1
A,2	− 31	4	7	10	14	18	11	5	− 3	− 61	− 26	− 2.2
A,3	− 33	2	4	8	13	17	7	2	− 7	− 73	− 60	− 5.0
A,4	− 35	− 0	3	6	13	17	3	− 3	− 10	− 86	− 92	− 7.7
A,5	− 37	− 2	1	6	12	18	− 1	− 7	− 14	− 99	− 123	− 10.3
A,6	− 38	0	6	12	19	23	5	− 7	− 14	− 94	− 88	− 7.4
A,7	− 33	12	17	24	29	36	35	10	− 9	− 76	45	3.8
A,8	− 10	36	38	39	41	46	57	52	27	− 5	321	27.0
A,9	12	59	60	61	62	65	71	73	66	163	692	58.2
A,10	360	554	554	554	554	554	554	554	554	2023	6815	143.3
2,3	− 47	− 11	− 8	− 5	− 1	0	− 11	− 17	− 25	− 135	− 260	− 21.9
2,4	− 49	− 12	− 10	− 6	− 2	− 1	− 14	− 20	− 27	− 144	− 285	− 24.0
7	− 98	− 20	− 13	− 6	1	7	− 13	− 40	− 53	− 276	− 511	− 21.5
8	− 83	− 4	2	9	15	22	16	− 11	− 39	− 228	− 301	− 12.7
9	− 100	21	37	56	74	91	48	28	− 14	− 242	− 1	− 0.0
10	− 82	117	134	151	170	186	127	93	49	− 67	878	21.3
11	− 78	176	194	212	231	246	170	127	83	128	1489	31.3
12	− 357	− 158	− 150	− 133	− 103	− 99	− 139	− 177	− 221	− 1089	− 2626	− 31.5
13	− 378	− 190	− 157	− 132	− 103	− 99	− 176	− 211	− 246	− 1195	− 2887	− 34.7
14	− 340	− 163	− 139	− 110	− 88	− 85	− 182	− 203	− 235	− 1106	− 2651	− 37.2
15	− 356	− 162	− 139	− 114	− 85	− 85	− 202	− 228	− 258	− 1188	− 2817	− 39.5
16	− 307	− 135	− 116	− 96	− 75	− 70	− 185	− 208	− 229	− 1037	− 2458	− 41.3
17	− 294	− 71	− 54	− 36	− 21	3	− 48	− 176	− 192	− 843	− 1732	− 29.1
18	− 138	45	55	64	74	103	147	36	− 69	− 345	− 28	− 0.6
19	− 41	143	148	155	163	182	227	218	98	− 16	1277	26.8
Win/Loss	− 2644	699	954	1235	1549	1777	1096	436	− 316	− 5306	− 520	− .5
%	− .3	9.1	12.4	16.1	20.1	23.1	14.2	5.7	− 4.1	− 17.2	− .5	− .5

PLAYER'S 2 CARD HAND

83

To accurately work out all the figures in chart No. 35 was an extremely complicated process. It required the aid of a high speed digital computer —the mathematician's friend, indeed. Rather than actually simulating the playing of billions of games of Blackjack, the law of probabilities was used to make direct computations. It was determined the best way to play each hand. Then, if for example, the results of hitting a 12 against a dealer 10 until the player obtained 17 or better was required, the computer was instructed to precisely calculate the probability of every possible card combination in conjunction with every possible dealer hole card and outcome. The results were then weighted according to the average expected frequency of each combination.

Adding it all up you can see from the bottom line that with correct basic stategy you will have the edge whenever the dealer shows a 2, 3, 4, 5, 6, 7, or 8. The dealer's weakest up card is a six giving you a 23 % edge. When the dealer has a ten showing you are at a 17% disadvantage. The overall result for basic strategy is shown as a loss of .5% making it a nearly even game. With a little bit of luck or a little bit of additional skill, you may come out ahead. More about this later.

Chart No. 35 is based on typical Las Vegas Strip rules where the dealer stands on all 17's and does not allow you to double down after splitting pairs. However, because of the enormous complexity of the computations for resplitting, the chart was prepared with the simplifying assumption that pairs cannot be resplit. Allowing that all pairs (except aces) can be resplit, which is the usual rule, gives the player an additional .1% in the multi-deck game. Thus, the actual figure for basic strategy for the typical Las Vegas Strip casino 4 deck game is -.4% rather than the -.5% shown.

If the dealer hits soft 17, which is typical in downtown Las Vegas casinos, you will lose about .2% more. If you are allowed to double down after splitting pairs you will win about .1% more. Finally, some casinos, such as those in Atlantic City, New Jersey have such good rules that correct basic strategy will actually give the player a slight edge. In spite of this, the Atlantic City casinos are raking in millions of dollars every month from their Blackjack tables. We trust that by learning the principles in this book you will be far less likely to be one of the contributors to the casino's winnings.

A note here for the proposition bettor: Suppose someone offered to give you a 10,9 as your hand against a dealer up card of 10 and deal the dealer's hole card and subsequent hits, if needed, randomly. The dealer would be required to stand, as usual, upon making 17 or better. Would you bet the 10,9 in this situation? How much would you expect to win or lose? The answers can be deduced from charts No. 34 and No. 35. Chart No. 34 shows that this situation will occur about 1455 times in 100,000 hands. Chart No. 35 shows that for those hands a net loss of 16 units occurs. Now $16/1455 = 1.1\%$ approximately, in favor of the dealer. Thus, you should not bet the 10,9 unless you like giving away 1.1% of your wager.

7

GOOD HANDS — BAD HANDS:
THEIR EFFECT ON BASIC STRATEGY

I have mentioned several times the use of Basic Strategy would allow you to play the house almost even. That is, by following all of the rules for hitting, standing, splitting and doubling as was suggested in the tables previously, you will, on average, neither win nor lose very much money if you bet the same amount on each hand.

> *Actually, you should expect to lose more hands than you win. However, if you will count a winning double-down as two hands won, a losing double-down as two hands lost, a winning blackjack as 1½ hands won, split pairs as two hands (or more, in case of a double down after a split) then you will, within a fraction, be winning about 50% of the time.*

Later on we will be discussing the use of systems which swing the odds in your favor.

Reference is once again made to Charts No. 34 and 35 in the preceding chapter. They dramatize the number of times you will get good and bad hands. I suppose someone might characterize a good hand as being one that wins. For our purpose, we define any given hand as being good or bad by the odds it has for becoming a winner. The figures in the right hand column of Chart No. 35 show the results for each hand as a percentage. Thus, by standing on 10,10 you will, on average, gain 58¢ for every dollar bet in this situation.

Please observe the amount of times within 100,000 hands you will be holding a hand 12 through 17. If you were to total these across against all of the Dealer's possible up cards in Chart No. 34, you would get a total of 42,798. This means your first two cards will total 12 to 17 just a little less than 43% of the time. Since the only way you can win with 12 to 17 is to either improve your hand or to have the Dealer bust, you will agree these are bad hands and you are going to get your share of bad hands. (But then again, so will the Dealer.)

The point here is to accept and recognize this probability of your share of bad hands. The secret is to know what to do about such adversities.

THE MOST IMPORTANT CARD ON THE TABLE

There can be seven players plus the Dealer at the table, all holding cards. Each, including yourself, having been dealt their first two cards, will be preoccupied with what their own total is, and that is as it should be. However, you are well on the way to being a good player when you recognize the most critical card on the table is the dealer's up-card.

Really think of it. It is this revealed card which sets everything in motion. It is the on/off switch for all of your decisions, and the absolute determinant for the entire game.

The reasons are obvious. The game begins with your two cards vs. the dealer's two cards. You now know the value of three of those cards. Wouldn't it be nice if you knew for sure the value of that covered card? Of course you can't know or there would be no game. You do know this however; it has to be one of 10 values. It is precisely this fact which brings about the business of PROBABILITIES. And it is specifically these probabilities which form the foundation for all strategies.

Here is where our friend the computer comes to our assistance. It has allowed me to set into motion the equivalent of billions of hands while accommodating all of the conditions that exist in a four deck game. Chart No. 36 which follows is the mathematical diagram of Dealer Probabilities. It is one of the most important charts in the book from the standpoint of justifying all of the recommendations for the basic strategy you must use when playing four deck Blackjack.

The figures 2 through Ace displayed vertically represent the Dealer's visible card. The probabilities of the Dealer making various totals are shown horizontally.

Let us now examine the implications of the figures shown on Chart No. 36 for they tell us a great deal. It is obvious were you to stand on any value of 12 to 16 against the Dealer's 2 for fear of busting by hitting, you would lose 65% of the time and win 35% of the games. Not very good odds. Putting it another way, were you to bet $5.00 for 100 games under these conditions, you would lose $325.00, win $175.00, for a net loss of $150.00.

On the other hand, the table clearly demonstrates the house vulnerability when the Dealer has a 4, 5 or 6 as his open card. Surely, we will want to maximize our opportunities at those times.

As you have discovered, there are many things we can do about all this.

CHART NO. 36

DEALER'S PROBABILITIES

(For Reference Only — Need Not be Learned)

Dealer Shows	17 or More	18 or More	19 or More	20 or More	21	Bust
2	65	51	37	24	12	35
3	63	49	36	24	12	37
4	60	47	35	23	11	40
5	58	46	34	22	11	42
6	58	41	31	20	10	42
7	74	37	23	15	7	26
8	76	63	27	14	7	24
9	77	65	53	18	6	23
10*	77	65	53	41	4	23
A*	83	65	46	27	8	17

*Figures shown are for case where dealer does not have a Blackjack.

ONE DECK, FOUR DECKS ... THE DIFFERENCE

Many of the major casinos in the world have switched to dealing from one deck to four decks. To my knowledge, most of the books previously published on the subject have concentrated on single deck strategies. Since the use of four or more decks appears to be growing, the relevance of showing and referencing the four deck strategy is apparent.

In order to accommodate those of our readers still interested in the strategy for single deck play, the differences have been noted within each of the chapters.

The history of how four deck play began is rather vague. One story has it originating at the beginning of casino operations in one of the Caribbean Islands. There was apparently a problem with collusion of native dealers with certain friends. To make it more difficult for such cheating to go on, one of the bright managers conceived the idea of four decks. Because so many cards were difficult to handle, they developed a plastic box from which the cards could be dealt to the players. From this crude beginning was developed the "shoe." This plastic device now in common use, holds the cards at 45° to the table and permits the Dealer to slide the cards to each of the players at accelerated speeds.

The news of this development was slow to be adopted by the Nevada casinos. It is sometimes difficult to change old habits. However, after Professor Thorp's book *Beat the Dealer* appeared in 1962 and produced a rash of "counters," some of the casino managements perceived that perhaps this island development of four decks might be a way to thwart this threat . . . and thus the emergence of four or more deck games.

The multi-deck game, however, also has some advantages for the players.* It does make it more difficult for a "mechanic" to operate. Mechanics are Dealers so agile in sleight of hand they can stack the deck. They were employed long ago by the criminal elements who had control of the early casinos. They insured the house would win by out and out cheating. It is almost impossible to cheat with four or more decks that have been well shuffled and put into the shoe. One other advantage is that clusters of wins tend to be sustained in multi-deck play.

As noted before, the use of four decks does place an additional burden on the system player. It requires him to make adjustments to his count for the number of cards remaining in the undealt decks.

I know many players who prefer four or more decks simply because it is a much faster game. Since there are fewer interruptions for shuffling, they like the greater "action" it provides.

---

*It should be remembered, however, multi-deck play is more advantageous to the casino. The calculations for Basic Strategy for one-deck indicate a .1% advantage for the player. In multiple decks, the house has about .4% edge. Some people consider this important. Others ignore this five/tenths of a percent difference in favor of the faster game.

10

THOSE BEAUTIFUL ACES

Whether you split them, double down with them, or get a blackjack with them, Aces are beautiful. Unfortunately, they are also the card which gives some players the most difficult time.

Mainly, this confusion is due to the Ace's dual personality. That is, you have the option of giving it a count of one or eleven. This is further complicated by the speed of the game. Some people just need more time to sort it out.

Remember our advice. You have the right to slow the game as much as you need to. If the alternate count of the Ace gives you a problem, take your time. The Dealer will wait.

I can't tell you how many times I have seen counts of 20 and even 21 passed by simply because the player did not recognize the eleven count of the Ace. For example, look at the following cards in sequence.

   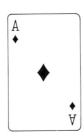

You and I may get 20 out of it. You'd be surprised how many people hit this hand thinking they have a count of 10.

Even more important than the missed count are those players who simply don't understand the "soft" count. Let's look at these two cards:

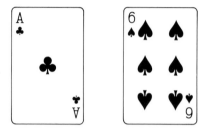

Obviously, these two cards may be counted as either 7 or 17. Some players, remembering you don't hit a 17 will stand. What an opportunity they are missing, particularly if the Dealer has an 8 or better showing. The advantage of any "soft" count is that you may hit with absolutely no possibility of busting. It's almost like getting a free bonus card.

How about these two cards:

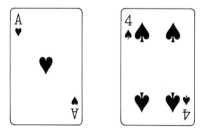

5 or 15, right? Right. Let's imagine the Dealer has a 6 showing. By the strategy already discussed, this would be a Double Down hand. But let's say you are not inclined to double your bet, what would you do? Some

players, remembering you don't hit a 15 against the Dealer's 6 would stand. How silly. Hit, for heaven's sake. You have several chances to improve your hand, and it's absolutely impossible to bust.

Consider this situation:

YOUR HOLDING   DEALER SHOWS

As was shown earlier, this hand would only win about 41% of the time. If you hit it you have several possibilities. If you get a 3 or deuce or another ace you would stand with a soft 21, 20, or 19, respectively. If you get a 10 you will then have a hard count of 18 and would stand. If you should get (horror of horrors!) a 4 to 8 you would hit again until you have a hard count of 17 or better. Your card sequence, on occasion, may look something like this:

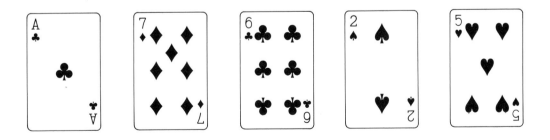

A 5 card 21!

Hitting the soft 18 against a dealer 10 will win about 43% of the time. Hitting soft 18 is also recommended against a dealer 9 and against a dealer ace. By hitting you either: (1) improve your hand immediately with an ace, deuce or trey; (2) still have an 18 if you get a ten; (3) have a further chance to improve your hand by further hitting should you get a 4 to 8; (4) reduce your hand to 17 should get you a 9.

Yes, Aces are beautiful . . . but only if you know what to do with them. If you have problems with Aces, work harder. Practice. Your Aces will produce more wins than any other card. Use them well; they are truly your friends.

11

THE CLOSE ONES

You will no doubt have noted how very marginal some of your decisions will have to be. For example, the hitting or standing of your hard 12 vs. the Dealer's 4 is shown as a +0 in favor of standing. What of your 16 vs. the Dealer's 10? After all, you will be faced with these two particular options approximately 25 times in every 1000 hands.

I have a friend, who while not a professional, is nevertheless a serious and highly successful player. He will play an average of 5 or 6 times a year, and his objective is always to be a big winner. I was curious as to what response he would have to this business of the marginal percentages. His answer went something like this.

> *"Given a choice between hit, stand or surrender, I would hit every time. I don't like the idea of playing defensively, and the word 'surrender' is not in my vocabulary. They go against my psyche. I just don't like giving the house an inch."*

Knowing he was a strict Basic Strategy player, I pointed out his gain in surrendering his 16 against a 10 would be 3%, he replied:

"I know Julian, but that is where I draw the line. I'll give them the percentage on that particular play rather than just hand over half my money. That sort of thing is bad for my attitude."

Where would you 'draw the line'? By strict, albeit narrow mathematics the strategy indicates surrender. Does my friend have a point? We will look more closely at these personal philosophies in our chapter on Money Management.

12

WHICH TABLE ... WHICH POSITION
WHAT TIME OF DAY?

The table you play at can be important. Several factors can influence your choice. First, what are the minimums and maximums. In this regard, you should understand that with the exception of the minimum, you can do pretty much the same thing at the $2.00 table as you can at the $5.00 or $25.00 table. That is, there is nothing to prevent you from betting $100.00 or more at the $2.00 or $5.00 tables.

Generally speaking, you will find a variance in the ability of the players at each of these tables. That is not to say you won't find excellent players at the $2.00 table, and poor ones at the $25.00 table. I have seen ridiculous decisions being made at the $100.00 table.

Where do you feel most comfortable? That must certainly be one of the important considerations in your choice. Now as to table-hopping. I do believe in cycles. That is, a Dealer can go along sort of up and down, with no particular pattern of good or bad cards. Then again, he can have a cycle of excessively good or bad luck. If a Dealer appears to be hitting everything in sight like pulling seven cards to a 21, or always turning up 10's as his face card, why not change tables? He obviously has got something going, why fight it. Remember, this could quickly change an hour from now. The point is, you have a right to look around. It might be worth while.

As to which position at the table you should play, again, that is a highly personal decision. You may have heard somewhere that 'first base' (the seat immediately to the Dealer's left which is dealt first) is better than 'third base' (the last one dealt).

Personally, I don't see a whole lot of difference. Those who prefer 'first base' believe it allows them to receive their cards before some of the players make their mistakes. This brings us to the entire question of your relationship with your co-players. Your attitude in this matter is most critical. For example. Let's say you are sitting at 'third base' (the last position). You have a count of 16, the Dealer has a 5 showing. Basic Strategy dictates you should stand. The player directly ahead of you has a count of 12. He too should stand. Instead, he hits and receives a 10; going bust. The Dealer turns up 15 as a result of his 5. He hits and receives a 4 for a total of 19. You lose. Obviously, if your co-player had stood as he was supposed to, the Dealer would have received that 10, and gone bust. You would have won that big bet! Are you mad? I should hope!

But wait, let's reverse the situation. Your co-player, hitting when he shouldn't receives a 6. The Dealer now gets the 10 for a bust. Had your co-player stayed with his 12 the Dealer would have received the 6 for a total of 21. It works both ways. You take your chances with your co-players. If you can look at it objectively, it really doesn't make any difference what they do as it all evens out.

There is, however, much irritation that occurs as a result of other players' lack of knowledge. It is to this extent that sitting alongside poor players can be damaging. I for one try to avoid that irritation as much as possible. I do so by trying never to play with more than two other players, or by leaving a table which is giving me a fit.

This in turn leads us into the subject of what time of day is best to play. I like the unbusy hours. These are usually mornings and afternoons, dinner time, during-the-showtime, and of course, the hours from 1 A.M. on. Again, a matter of personal preference and your own schedule.

It's a good idea not to play more than a couple of hours at a time. You should walk away to stretch your legs and give your mind a break. Most major casinos in the U.S. operate 24 hours a day. They will still be there when you return. All of the above should be followed unless you are on a big win streak. Never leave when everything is going your way. This sort of thing does not happen that frequently. Enjoy it to the hilt when it does.

On the other hand, don't be afraid to quit when it's going the other way, either for a few hours or for the rest of the day. There's always tonight or tomorrow or the next time you come. This is how to be a smart and tough player. Play sparsely when you are losing, never quit when you are winning.

13

PRACTICE

I have an uncommon respect for you, dear Reader. By the mere act of purchasing this book, I feel I know a little bit about you. First, you believe in researching your subject, and in investigating other points of view. All of this with the idea you can learn something that will help you. Next, you have a seriousness of purpose that demands as much knowledge about an undertaking as is possible. It is within this context that the following remarks are made.

The title of this chapter is deceptive. After all, what is all this effort of yours about? Some people go to the casino with the idea of "losing a few dollars." They view the activity as though it was part of the price of the vacation, like the air fare or hotel room. The casino management loves such people.

But whatever the attitude, there is one thing all players of all persuasions have in common. They will be winning or losing real money, real American dollars. They may not be worth as much these days; nevertheless they are the coin of the realm.

In no other of life's experiences will you find people giving it away as easily as they do in the casino. Ask anyone who's doing just that and they'll answer, "Well, it's worth the price of admission, and I am having fun."

I must admit to you that I too have been known to give it away, but not without a fight. If they beat me, it will not be because I haven't battled them for every inch. I'll work for every tenth of a percent I can get. I play to win. I hate to lose.

That's what I think this exercise is all about. That's what these charts are all about. To be absolutely blunt, you'll get out of this book exactly what you put into it. As long as I've used so many hackneyed phrases, I might as well use one more. You can lead a reader to Basic Strategy but you can't make the reader practice it.

Being an eternal optimist, I'm assuming I've reached you. That like me, the last thing you want to do is give your money away. In fact, and again like me, you'd actually like to win some money, as much as possible. What then? Practice! Dull and time consuming practice. The only reward I can promise you is your development into a good "tough" player.

I like the word "tough." It's Dealer and Pit Boss parlance for a player who doesn't make stupid mistakes. It's their way of communicating that this is a player who's done his homework, who knows the score, and because of that, will give the house a tough time.

At first I liked the idea of being considered a tough player. It gave me self-esteem. I was flattered. It was an ego trip knowing they knew I knew.

Frankly, that feeling has long since gone. Instead, it really doesn't matter to me what they think. What does matter, is whether I win or lose. If being tough helps me win, you wouldn't believe how tough I can become.

We've now come full circle back to our word "practice." Perhaps you have already spent some time with the various charts. You may even feel you know and understand them. O.K. then, it's humility time. There are four "homework" pages at the end of this book. I suggest you make a number of copies so you may continue testing yourself. Check your answers. Feel humble? Are you surprised at how much there is to learn? Most people are.

It's a good idea to check yourself in this manner from time to time, particularly the week before you go on your trip. Certainly, it would be far more interesting to test by practicing with four actual decks. The problem is, some of the combinations do not appear very often and there is a tendency to forget.

I think you will be very happy you spent as much time learning the Basic Strategy as you have. You will feel a little strange when you actually get to the casino. But this should not last more than half an hour. After that, you will feel right at home. All your work will have paid off through the self-confidence you feel in the full knowledge you know what you are doing.

14

SELF DISCIPLINE

This night you can do no wrong. Your 14's become 20's, and the Dealer is busting all over the place on your Double Downs. This can and will happen. But look out. It can change in minutes. Blackjack is one of the most humbling experiences I know. You can go from flying high to being completely flattened. And frankly, humility is not a bad virtue with which to approach the game.

Please do not misunderstand. Humility is not antithetical to confident and aggressive strategy. Rather, it compliments the latter by insuring a continuous vigil of the circumstances.

A good Blackjack player is a combination of the development of the strategy skills, and a cultivated awareness of the psychological effects which are constantly interacting. This chapter will concern itself with the second of these attainments.

It seems like every taxicab driver in the State of Nevada was once a tremendously big winner who fell on hard times, and therefore had to drive a cab to make a living. He will regale you with stories just like that . . . perhaps of a cousin, or a friend. The ending is always the same. True or not, such stories dramatize the need for a disciplined approach, a self-inquiry of goals and objectives.

Most people cannot identify with such extremes. They will not allow themselves to be either big winners or big losers. Nevertheless, this is just a matter of degree. The principles are the same, and well worth our contemplating.

I don't know under what circumstances you are reading this chapter. I must assume you are comfortable and that the environment is neither hostile nor frenetic. Now transfer yourself if you will, to the surroundings of the casino. A whirl of activity. Hundreds of people congregated around dozens of tables. All sharing the same experience, the fun and excitement of gambling. You begin. Like your first steps into the pool, the water feels cold and threatening. But pretty soon you get into the swim of it. It feels comfortable and invigorating.

Believe me, it is different than being at home. After a day or two, you fall into the rhythm of the place. You have adjusted to this new world, and as one of its new citizens, begin to take on some of its values. You might be surprised at the subtle changes in judgment you experience. This is your vacation, and you are enjoying every minute of it!

I have no quarrel with any of this. After all, this is exactly why I go. On the other hand, you must recognize these changes are occurring to you. There could be serious consequences if you don't. This is not particularly a caution message that you may lose more money than you planned. I have often lost myself, but still come home convinced I had had a good time. The reason? I had maintained control, and knew at all times what I was doing.

This last statement may appear pollyannish to you. Losing is losing, and no one enjoys it. That's true. However, you start out knowing you can win or lose. If you have studied your strategy, if you have played well and maintained control of your emotions, then losing becomes a fact of life you can comfortably accommodate, like the little rain that must fall.

The same can be true of winning. Some people win a little and quit for fear they might give it back. Later, they remonstrate with themselves for quitting too soon rather than winning more than they had. Some win a lot, continue to play, and end up giving it back, and then some. They too, will not forgive themselves.

See the problem? Know thyself. Look, this is no sermon. But you better know what's going on. I can't advise you what to do, only some of the things you shouldn't do. I can tell you my discipline; maybe this will help you prepare your own.

> I DO NOT set a ceiling on winning.
> I DO NOT play when I am tired.
> I DO NOT drink when I am playing.
> I DO NOT go against my strategies.
> I DO NOT chase my money by betting more
> than originally planned.

I DO NOT play hunches.

I DO NOT forget Blackjack is a serious game.

I DO NOT ever forget I can just walk away.

I DO set a ceiling on the amount I will lose.

I DO rest and relax between sessions.

I DO exercise each day.

I DO get a set of rules for the casino where I'm playing.

I DO change tables if I continue to lose.

I DO quit for the day if I still continue to lose.

I DO forgive myself if I've done something stupid.

I DO maintain strategy under all conditions.

I DO bet more when I'm winning.

I DO bet less when I'm losing.

There you have mine. Why not take a moment to do yours? Allow me to give you one clue. Be yourself. Be the person you like, and with whom you feel comfortable. Don't be brash or fearless if you are by nature not so. A phony macho is self-defeating.

Contrarily, you have every reason to be self-assured. You've learned the odds, the strategies. You've practiced well. You understand what losing is all about. You can be resolute without being vain, and confident without being complacent. You can hit that 15 when you have to because you know it's the right thing to do.

15

MONEY MANAGEMENT

We come now to the most controversial, and certainly the most personal of decisions which need to be made when playing Blackjack.

Since it ranks in importance alongside Basic Strategy in determining your winnings and losses, it is difficult to understand why the subject has hardly at all been discussed by other writers.

Variations of this story have made the rounds for years. It seems on one particular evening, a young lady picked up the dice at the craps table. The results were nothing but spectacular. She threw fourteen sevens in a row! She won $26.00. A young man at the other end of the table won $16,000.00 betting on her. How is this possible? Easy. Every time the young lady won, she pulled two dollars, leaving her original two dollars for the next roll. In contrast, the young man let his money ride. That is, he didn't pull or drag anything back. One hundred became two hundred. Two hundred became four hundred and so forth. This is called parlaying, and it has a vital bearing on the results you achieve.

Since we have previously said the probabilities are that in strict units of hands played, the house will win more hands than you do, how is it possible for you to be a winner? An important part of the answer lies in money management. We have already discussed two of the ways. Specifically, the ability to double your bet when splitting pairs or doubling down. The last and most important way is by parlaying.

As in the craps game example, it is all but impossible to win a lot of money without parlaying. Even that young lady's incredible performance netted just $26.00. Let's look a little more closely at how parlaying works.

We'll use chips as examples. The chip may be of any value you wish to assign. Your first bet is one chip. You win, and now have two. You must decide whether to drag one or to let the two ride. Suppose you decide on the latter. You win again, and now have four. Let's stop right here and see what happened.

First, you have been paid at the odds of 3 to 1. The odds against your winning two hands in a row are about 3 to 1. Remember, however, that one of the two chips you were betting the second time was actually casino money,* and had you lost, you would have lost only one of your own chips.

What now? Let the four ride? O.K. After all, only one of those is yours. You win again. You now have eight chips. You have been paid 7 to 1. The odds of winning three in a row is 7 to 1.

Let's really dream. On this third hand, you get an opportunity to double down. You do so by placing four of your own chips alongside the four of

---

*Properly, once you've won any chips its *your* money, but many players take the view that until such time as you lock up such profits you are playing with the casino's money.

your original bet. Lo and behold you win your double down as the Dealer goes bust. You have now a total of sixteen chips, all of which started with just one of your own. This is the way lots of money is won on a relatively small investment.

Suppose you had lost that final double-down bet. You would have been out five chips. Not a bad bet. You are risking five to win sixteen at a time when the Dealer is most vulnerable. (He had to be or you would not have been doubling.)

This scenario dramatically illustrates the options you have in money management. Your decisions in this regard will determine the size of your winnings and losses. How do you decide? Are there any sure-fire guidelines? I'm afraid not. Odds are odds. You decide to defy them or you don't.

Let me try to help. The first factor is your own personality. Recall in the last chapter we discussed the virtues of being true to yourself. If you are conservative by nature and feel uncomfortable with that third bet, don't do it. This isn't just one bet we're talking about, it's an attitude, a money management strategy. These are the same kind of decisions you will have to make all the time you are playing . . . hundreds of times. It certainly isn't worth doing anything which will contribute to your distress or discomfort.

How about the second bet? Would you be comfortable with that one? There are also intermediates. You could go to the third bet and take some out. One thing is certain. You must do something like parlaying or the house will grind it out of you. They will on probability win more hands than you do. You must find some compensatory plan to counteract. In other words, they win more hands, you win more money.

Apart from your personality consideration, there is one additional input which should affect your money management strategy. That is, the way the cards are running at any particular time. Call it luck, cycle or anything you please. There does appear to be this element of cluster which shows up from time to time. Typical patterns might look like this:

Your strategy should be to go with the pitch. Remember that old truism, bet more when you're winning and less when you are losing. Work at your sensitivity for recognizing these clusters and act accordingly.

You should also consider increasing your betting in direct proportion to your winnings. The initial bet in any given series should equal approximately 2-5% of those winnings . . . if you want to win big. You should keep this up only as long as your winning streak is continuing. Retreat quickly when you sense the trend has reversed. Your parlay strategy, or any of your strategies for that matter, should never change just because there is more money on the table. After all, these strategies are what got you there; they should not be compromised by the amount of money at stake.

Contrarily, you should never chase your losses by betting more in order to catch up. This is suicidal. If you find yourself in a losing cluster, ride it out. Keep your bets to an absolute minimum until this cycle is reversed. If it sustains itself, either change tables, quit for a few hours, or even for the day. Your opportunities will most certainly come another time.

I hope you have ascertained from all of the preceding remarks on money management that apart from learning your Basic Strategy, it is the single most important determinant of the results you achieve. Let me anticipate some of your questions.

Q.   How much in real money should my first bet be?

A.   That depends on your budget. For example, assume you have decided the maximum amount you are prepared to lose is $500.00. You will then want to consider an initial bet of 2% or $10.00. A more conservative bet would be $5.00. This is not a bad idea until you see how the cards are going.

Q.   You said I could parlay once or twice; how about the third time?

A.   Nothing stops you from parlaying 12 times. You should remember, however, the longer you go, the greater are the odds and the risk. For myself, I will almost always parlay the first win; and will parlay the second time if I feel the shoe is going my way. I personally never go beyond that.

Q.   Assume I have won a cluster of two or three ($5.00 = $10.00 = $20.00 or $5.00 = $10.00 = $20.00 = $40.00). What should I do then?

A.   You start over with your $5.00 bet. There are exceptions. Suppose you feel you have a busting dealer on your hands. Graduate your initial bet, of course, but be sure to retreat to your original bet when the cards level out.

Q. When should I increase the amount of my first bet?

A. I assume, like most people, you will be playing in sessions. That is, you will play for a couple of hours, then relax for a while; lunch, dinner, swim, etc. You will want to use these intervals to re-evaluate. If your winnings have been considerable, you will certainly want to increase your initial bet. If the winnings are small, or if you are actually losing, you will want to retain the original amount.

PROGRESSIVE BETTING*

The advanced player may wish to consider progressive money management. Please note this method is to be used with great caution and discrimination. It is not for everyone. The objective is to maximize your winnings in a relatively short period of time, and to do so during a streak of winning hands. The negative side of this system is it can materially reduce your staying power since you are in fact re-investing your winnings. Here's how it works. Your goal is to reach a maximum bet of 10 times your original wager as soon as possible...and stay there. Using one unit of whatever value you determine, you would proceed as follows. Bet one and win. Bet two and win. Pull one (your original bet) and bet three. You win. Bet six, you win. Pull two and let the ten ride. You have at this point taken out three units and now have your maximum bet going. If you

---

*Progressive betting should be used only with great caution. In fact, its only use should be when you are certain you are in the middle of a real streak. The danger in accelerating your betting in this manner is it reduces your staying power. That is, you are exposing more of your winnings so that sustained losses quickly deplete the gains achieved from a moderate streak. The safest course is to conservatively build and establish your reserves via the basic parlay cadence, i.e., bet one and win, bet two and win, start over with one. Let experience and insight be your guide, but beware of over-exuberance and lack of humility.

win this bet, take out ten and continue with ten. Keep this up as long as your good fortune continues. You *must* start over whenever there is a break in the cycle. The number of units at which you re-start is determined by the amount of your winnings and whether you believe your streak of winning hands is continuing. The secret is your ability to recognize a streak as close to its beginning as possible, and the end of it as soon as possible so you may retreat quickly. Any wins of double down or splitting hands simply accelerate the progression. Personally, I use a combination of the basic parlaying strategy previously detailed together with progressive when I sense a first class streak is occurring. As you can see, any number of variations is possible. Primarily, you must recognize the tremendous importance of skillful money management. The agility and imagination with which you handle your betting is what will make you a great Black Jack player.

DEVELOP THAT SIXTH SENSE

I have alluded earlier to the word "sensitivity." Frankly, that is the most important word in my Black Jack dictionary. I caution you, however, sensitivity is a developed skill. Unless you are unique, sensitivity is developed with experience. One might liken it to jogging or lifting weights. You cannot run miles or lift hundreds of pounds starting out. These are skills that accrue from practice and doing. The sensitivity I'm talking about is a fine tuning to the particular shoe or dealer. A sixth sense, if you will, of when the circumstances are favoring the player. If the dealer is constantly showing you ten-valued cards, get out of there. He is forcing you to continually bet your stiffs, and giving you few opportunities for doubling down.

There is no way you can win against a dealer like that. Try to take maximum advantage when the opposite is true. Good money management is the ultimate strategy; it demands your most careful consideration.

NOTE:

The previous comments on money management represent a popular view. For a game such as dice, for example, when played honestly with good equipment, there would be no mathematical basis for such an approach — the dice have no memory. However, in multi-deck Blackjack there is a mathematical basis to substantiate, at least in part, the indicated approach. In multi-deck Blackjack when you win, you are more likely to have won from a pack that was rich in high valued cards. Once the pack becomes significantly rich in high cards it will tend to stay that way for several hands. Thus, there will be a tendency for wins to cluster at times in a more significant manner than pure randomness would suggest. In Blackjack, until such times as the pack is shuffled, the cards do have a memory and we must strive to take advantage of this fact.

16

OF PIT BOSSES AND DEALERS

I personally would not wish to be either one. On the other hand, I'm sure they would not want to have anything to do with computers. Before we speak of them as people, however, let's discuss their participation in the game, and most importantly, how they may affect your winnings and losings.

Many people believe, even after playing for awhile, that the Dealer can somehow directly affect the outcome of the game. For all intents and purposes, that is not true. The Dealer operates under a mandated set of rules from which it is impossible for him or her to deviate. The most important of these is to hit his own count until he reaches 17 (soft and/or hard depending on the particular casino). Your count at any time, or that of any other player, has nothing to do with this decision. The Dealer has absolutely no choices and no options during the game. He is obligated to shuffle, deal, keep count, to take your money when you lose, and to pay you when you win. The Dealer cannot advise or consent. Without being critical or demeaning, the Dealer is nothing more than a machine, programmed to perform these specific functions while being completely oblivious to the results. This non-involvement does lead to some strange manifestations which we shall later discuss.

Pit Bosses, the men and women clustered between the rows of Blackjack tables, also have nothing to do with the outcome of the game. (We are assuming play is in one of the major casinos in the U.S. where cheating has sort of gone out of style.) Their responsibility is to supervise play, rotate Dealers, record the winnings and losings at each table, watch for counters, daubers, and other kinds of trickery on the part of players, and to act as arbiters in the event of a dispute. The spotters who watch from peepholes in the ceiling are doing pretty much the same.

I for one cannot quarrel with this policing. Fair is fair. Casinos have been preyed upon by every kind of schemer, and are taken for millions of dollars annually by the most ingenius kind of conniving. Stories are rampant about the most unlikely devices imaginable. Rube Goldberg-like electronic paraphanelia, strapped to the body in unbelievable ways. Signaling schemes, invisible inks, crimpers; all being continually re-invented as ways to cheat the casino. Some of these methods even involve a conspiratorial Dealer.

Some people might say, "Who cares? They can certainly afford it." I won't comment on this. It merely explains why the casino has so many 'policemen'.

Every book on Blackjack I've read has commented on both Dealer and Pit Boss. In the main, the authors' remarks have been acrimonious, to say the least. Their descriptions range from 'stupid' and 'arrogant' all the way to 'nasty' and 'belligerent'. I must say I too have met all four of these prototypes.

As in any group, however, it is difficult to categorize all Pit Bosses and all Dealers as having all or some of these attributes. In an attempt to be kind, I will just say that only the majority are that way.

You know how you feel when you go to an expensive restaurant, and the Maitre d' gives you that haughtier than thou treatment. And then the waiter. He acts like you should be eating a Big Mac instead of taking up his time in this gourmet heaven in which he has been blessed to work. That is exactly the attitude of many of the Casino personnel.

Maybe the fact we flock there by the millions produces this disregard for our rights. We become faceless. After all, this week's crop will be replaced by another. What does it matter?

I have noted lately the smallest of attempts to ameliorate this condescending behavior. Too bad they are that way. If they are going to take our money, they ought to at least be nice. Even if we take some of theirs, they should be nice.

The only reason I spend any time at all discussing them is they can have an effect on your play. We've discussed one of the ways, the fast dealer. By far the more insidious threat, however, is the one of intimidation. You can sit for days if you are losing, and no pit boss will come near you. But then you win. You begin winning with regularity. Here they come. The approach is most usually a smile, then an introduction. Ever so congenially the pit boss will want to know who you are and where you come from. You don't have to tell them, you know. I usually return their smile and handshake, however, "Yeah, Hi, I'm Tommy from Brockton." That's as far as it will go . . . unless you keep winning. Suddenly, you have a friend. They will observe your play, at first in a disinterested way, then more intensely.

Don't be intimidated by all this attention. Remember, they are doing the policing job we described. They have to decide whether you are 'legit'.or not. Even if you see several pit bosses discussing a subject which is obviously you, pay no attention. By no means let it distract you from your game. You're doing what you came to do, which is to win. You are doing it honestly. So just go about your business while they do the worrying.

Here's the kicker, believe it or not. When you start winning, the Dealer expects to be tipped. Would you believe this? O.K., it's been going on for years. I must tell you I have also tipped. In most instances, though, it's been not just when I am winning, but when the Dealer has worked at being cordial, and when he doesn't act like it's the end of the world because I've won a few dollars.

A lot of people tip because they believe it will keep their luck going, or that the Dealer will somehow or other help them. It's a highly personal decision.

If you are going to tip, there are two ways of doing so. The first is to simply hand the Dealer a chip. The second way is to place that chip to the leading edge of your box, directly in front of the chips you are betting. This signifies you are betting the Dealer's tip for him on your next hand. If you win, the Dealer gets two chips as his tip. If you lose, all chips go to the house. The obvious reason for doing this is to somehow influence the

124

Dealer to give him greater incentive for dealing you good cards. Really, I hope you won't count on such kind of wishful thinking. If you are inclined to tip, give him the chip.

To summarize, you are the 'customer'. You have as much right to win as you do to lose. Pit Bosses and Dealers comes in every size and sex, and in every attitude and demeanor. Your best bet is to have them be as faceless to you as you are to them. Be cordial and sociable, but never forget why you are there.

17

THE BRAUN POINT-COUNT SYSTEM

If you really want to work at playing winning Blackjack, you should learn how to use one of the many winning count systems available. This chapter shall devote itself to my own system. It is offered here for the first time. The next section will examine some of the other systems being offered.

However, Dear Reader, you should be forewarned count systems are not for everyone. They demand an unbelievable amount of dedication, and untold hours of diligent practice and application.

By far the greatest proportion of this Report has been concerned with Basic Strategy. For it is that information which must be understood by everyone who ever plans to play Blackjack.

What follows should only be attempted by the very few who are seriously inclined to master the skill of counting. As you read through, therefore, remember that Basic Strategy of itself is a powerful advantage, one that you will share with a comparatively small group of players. Accordingly, if you elect to pass by the small additional advantage counting can give you, don't feel badly. You've already learned enough to play very well.

It should be apparent that when the deck or multi-deck pack is richer than usual in tens or aces it will favor the player. Not only will the player get more Blackjacks, but he will have more winning double-downs, and in general, less bad hands. Therefore, the prime purpose of a count system is to help in evaluating when the pack is rich in high cards so that a player may bet more in those situations. This is the first aspect of a winning count system.

The second is its use for improving the play of the hand. This involves considerably more effort. First, you would have to memorize a chart of indexes associated with the system. Then, in addition to keeping certain types of running counts as you observe the cards, you would have to compute an index value from these counts. The computed index is then compared to the memorized chart value to determine the proper play. Sound like a lot of work? We told you so. However, with a considerable amount of practice many players have learned to do it very well. Professional players find it well worth the effort. Let us now take a look at the system.

The first part involves keeping a running point count. The point count values are as follows:

CARD	COUNT	CARD	COUNT
2	+1	8	0
3	+1	9	0
4	+1	10	-1
5	+1	Jack	-1
6	+1	Queen	-1
7	0	King	-1
		Ace	-1

After the cards are shuffled you start with a count of zero. For every small card (2, 3, 4, 5, or 6) you see, add one point to your running count. For every ace or ten valued card, you subtract one from your running count. Ignore all 7's, 8's, and 9's.

For many playing decisions you will need to convert the running count to an appropriate index value and compare it to a memorized table value to determine your best strategy. This is the second and most complicated part of the system. For an appropriate index value we shall use the COUNT PER DECK concept. A running count of +8 with two decks remaining is equivalent to a running count of +4 with one deck remaining or a running count of +2 with half a deck remaining. All are equivalent to a count of +4 per deck. To obtain the count per deck simply divide the running count by the estimated number of decks remaining. An approximation will suf-

CHART NO. 37

Playing the Stiffs with
The 4 Deck Braun System

	DEALER SHOWS									
YOU HAVE	2	3	4	5	6	7	8	9	10	ACE
18 or more	S	S	S	S	S	S	S	S	S	S
17	S	S	S	S	S	S	S	S	S	—7
16	—9	—11	—12	—13	—13	9	7	5	0	8
15	—6	—7	—8	—10	—10	10	10	8	4	9
14	—4	—5	—7	—8	—8	16	H	H	H	13
13	—1	—2	—4	—5	—5	H	H	H	H	H
12	3	2	0	—2	—1	H	H	H	H	H

fice. In border line situations a slight error may result in the wrong choice of optimum strategy, but the difference in average percentage gain or loss will be small.

Stand if the count per deck is larger than the table entry. Hit if the count per deck is less than the table entry. Stand or hit, as you prefer, when the count per deck equals the number in the table. Note that basic strategy applies where there is no number in the table.

The most important numbers to learn are the numbers between -5 and +5 as these will occur the most frequently. Learn these first. I have generally only shown table values between -16 and +16. Since values beyond this range infrequently occur I do not think such indexes are worth presenting.

Also, to correctly play the extreme indexes increases the probability of your being barred. Suppose, for example, that you hold a hard 17 against a dealer 10, the count per deck is an amazing -25 (lots of little cards available) and you know the table value is -22. (This is the correct table value, but I deliberately omitted it.) If you correctly hit and get, say, a 3 or 4 with the pit boss watching he is apt to regard you as a smart player. Depending on how closely you are being scrutinized, it may at times pay you to give up a few "smart" plays.

CHART NO. 38

Playing the Hard Double Downs
with The 4 Deck Braun System

DEALER SHOWS

YOU HAVE	2	3	4	5	6	7	8	9	10	ACE
11	—12	—13	—14	—14	—16	—10	—7	—5	—5	1
10	—9	—10	—11	—12	—14	—7	—5	—2	4	4
9	1	—1	—3	—5	—6	3	8			
6,2 or 5,3	14	9	6	4	2	14				
4,4	15	9*	6*	4*	8**	14				
7			12	9	10					
4,2			16	13	16					
3,2				13						

Double down if the count per deck is higher than the table value. Do not double down if there is no entry.

*Holding 4,4 against a dealer 3,4,or 5:
- a) If you are not allowed to double down after splitting use the table values shown.
- b) If you are allowed to double down after splitting, never double down on a holding of 4,4 versus a dealer 3,4 or 5. Instead, consider splitting using the appropriate table value in table 41.

**Holding 4,4 against a dealer 6:
- a)   If you are not allowed to double down after splitting, then double down if the count per deck exceeds 2.
- b)   If you are allowed to double down after splitting, split the 4's against a six if the count per deck is greater than -1 and less than or equal to 8. If its greater than 8, double down.

Note: Depending on how closely you are being scrutinized it may be wise to omit the ''smart'' plays of doubling down on holdings of 5 to 7.

CHART NO. 39

Playing the Soft Double Downs
with the Four Deck Braun System

DEALER SHOWS

YOU HAVE	2	3	4	5	6	7	8	9	10	ACE
A,10*	14	12	10	8	8	S				
A,9	10	9	7	5	5	14				
A,8	9	5	3	1	1	16				
A,7	1	—3	—7	—9	—11	S				
A,6	1	—5	—8	—11	—14	H				
A,5	H	4	—4	—8	—14	H				
A,4	H	6	—1	—6	—10	H				
A,3	14	7	1	—3	—6	H				
A,2	13	7	3	0	—3	H				

Double down if your count per deck exceeds the value in the table. *The (A,10) is not a Blackjack. These values are to be used for possibly doubling down on (A,10) resulting from obtaining an ace on a ten after splitting tens. Although this is a mathematically correct play in appropriately ten rich decks, this is another one of those "smart" plays that you may want to omit.

Standing or hitting with the four deck Braun System when holding a soft hand. There is only one table value to learn: Holding a soft 18 against a dealer ace, hit if your count per deck is less than 1. For other soft hands use the previous table where appropriate and follow basic strategy where the previous table does not apply.

Insurance: When the dealer shows an ace and you are offered insurance, you should make the wager that the dealer has a ten in the hole if the count per deck exceeds 2.

CHART NO. 40

SPLITTING PAIRS WITH THE 4 DECK BRAUN SYSTEM

Doubling down not permitted after splitting

DEALER SHOWS

YOU HAVE	2	3	4	5	6	7	8	9	10	ACE
A,A	—13	—13	—14	—15	—16	—11	—10	—9	—10	—5
10,10	10	8	6	5	4	13				
9,9	—2	—4	—5	—6	—6	7	—10	—11		5
8,8	SP	SP	SP	SP	SP	SP	SP	SP	6B	—13
7,7	—12	—13	—16	—17	SP	SP				
6,6	4	0	—3	—5	—8					
4,4										
3,3	8	3	—3	—4	—16	12B				
2,2	7	2	—4	—6	—13	SP				

CHART NO. 41

Doubling down is permitted after splitting

DEALER SHOWS

YOU HAVE	2	3	4	5	6	7	8	9	10	ACE
A,A	—13	—13	—14	—15	—16	—11	—10	—9	—10	—5
10,10	10	8	6	5	4	13				
9,9	—3	—5	—6	—7	—8	3	—10	—11		4
8,8	SP	SP	SP	SP	SP	SP	SP	SP	9B	—13
7,7	—12	—13	—16	—17	SP	SP	2			
6,6	—2	—4	—6	—8	—11					
4,4		8	4	0	—1					
3,3	—1	—6	—9	—10	—16	SP				
2,2	—4	—6	—8	—10	—14	SP	6			

If a number is shown, split if the count per deck is greater than that number. NOTE: If the number is followed by a B, read in reverse - in this case split if the count per deck is below the number. Do not split in the situations for which no entry is shown.

CHART NO. 42

Braun 4 Deck Count System modifications if Dealer hits soft 17

DEALER SHOWS

You Have	6	A	
Soft 18	Stand	Hit	
Hard 17	Stand	5	
Hard 16	—15	4	Stand if the count per deck is larger than the number shown.
Hard 15	—12	5	
Hard 14	—9	9	
Hard 13	—6	Hit	
Hard 12	—3	Hit	
Hard 7	9		
A,7	—13		Double down if the count per deck exceeds the number shown.
A,6	—16		
A,5	—16		
Case I: 9,9	—8	4	Split the pair of 9's if the count per deck exceeds the number shown.
Case II: 9,9	—10	2	

Case I: Double down NOT permitted after pair splitting.
Case II: Double down IS permitted after paid splitting.

The numbers in the previous tables assume the dealer stands on all 17's. If the dealer hits soft 17 this affects principally the situations where the dealer shows an Ace or a 6. If the dealer shows an Ace and hits soft 17 he will tend to make a somewhat better hand. However, when showing a 6 and holding soft 17 the dealer will tend not to gain because had he stood, his hand would have already beat the stiffs that most players will stand on in this situation. Only the modifications to the previous tables are shown here.

CHART NO. 43

Late surrender with the 4 Deck Braun System

DEALER SHOWS

You Have	8	9	10	Ace
17	Stand	10	10	
10,6	5	0	—3	—2
9,7	5	0	—3	—2
8,8	Split	10	2	Split
15	7	2	0	1
14*	9	5	3	5
13	13	9	6	9

If the casino offers the "late surrender" option throw in your hand giving up half your bet if the count per deck exceeds the number in the table.

*Holding 7,7 the appropriate numbers are 1 less than those shown for the other 14's.

CHART NO. 44

Early surrender with the 4 Deck Braun System

DEALER SHOWS		
You Have	10	Ace
2,2	15	1
2,3	12	0
Hard 6	11	—2
Hard 7	14	—3
Hard 8	No	10
Hard 12	8	—5
Hard 13	3	—8
Hard 14	—0.5	—10
7,7	—2	—12

DEALER SHOWS		
You Have	10	Ace
Hard 15	—3	—11
Hard 16	—6	—14
8,8	—2	—14
Hard 17	5	Always
A,2	No	13
A,3	No	9
A,4	16	7
A,5	15	5
A,6	No	6

Where you have the opportunity to surrender the hand before the dealer receives or looks at the hole card you should surrender against a dealer 10 or Ace if the count per deck exceeds the table entry. Against a dealer 8 or 9 use the previous chart. I am indebted to Dr. Peter Griffin of California State University for much of the data in these charts.

If you play this four deck count system in games where 80% of the shoe is dealt out before reshuffling you will gain about 1% profit relative to the money wagered if you vary your bets from about 1 to 4 units in accordance with the count.

The following statistics may be of interest. When using this sytem approximately 9.4% of the starting hands should be doubled and 2.2% of the hands should be split. On the doubled hands about 55% will be won, 38% lost, and 7% tied. On the non-doubled hands about 42.5% are won, 48.8% lost, and 8.7% tied. Proper insurance bets occur infrequently - only about 2 out of 11 times when the dealer shows an ace should insurance be taken.

With very little error, the four-deck system presented here also applies to games with more than four decks.

I have been frequently asked for my one deck system. So even though this book is primarily about the multi-deck game of Blackjack, I present on the following pages, as a bonus, my one deck system.

THE BRAUN ONE DECK COUNT SYSTEM

The same running count as used before is used here. After the cards are shuffled you start with a count of zero. For every 2, 3, 4, 5 or 6 that you see you add one point to the running count. For every ace or ten valued card that you see you subtract one from your running count. Ignore all 7's, 8's, and 9's.

To obtain the count per deck it will be more convenient to multiply by a "convenient multiplier" rather than to divide by the number of decks remaining. Here is a table of convenient multipliers:

Approximate number of cards remaining:

| 43 | 39 | 35 | 31 | 26 | 21 | 17 | 13 |

Convenient Multiplier:

| 6/5 | 4/3 | 3/2 | 5/3 | 2 | 2.5 | 3 | 4 |
| (1 + 1/5) | (1 + 1/3) | (1 + 1/2) | (1 + 2/3) | | (2 + 1/2) | | |

Example: The running count is 6 and you estimate that about 39 cards remain unseen. Since the convenient multiplier 4/3 is, of course, 1 + 1/3, I think of this as adding an extra 1/3 of the running count to get the count per deck. Thus, 6 + 1/3 of 6 is 6 + 2 = **8**, the count per deck.

CHART NO. 45

Playing the Stiffs with the Braun
One Deck Count System

DEALER SHOWS

YOU HAVE	2	3	4	5	6	7	8	9	10	ACE
18 or more	S	S	S	S	S	S	S	S	S	S
17	S	S	S	S	S	S	S	S	S	−9
16	−9	−11	−13	−14	−11	13	11	4	0	7
15	−5	−7	−9	−10	−11	13	14	8	4	8
14	−3	−5	−7	−9	−9	14	H	H	H*	12
13	0	−2	−4	−6	−5	H	H	H	H	H
12	4	2	0	−2	−1	H	H	H	H	H

Stand if the count per deck is larger than the table entry. Hit if the count per deck is less than the table entry. Stand or hit, as you prefer, when the count per deck equals the number in the table.

*Holding 7,7 versus a dealer 10 stand if the count per deck exceeds −1.5.

Insurance

Take insurance whenever your running count is +2 or more. Take insurance with a running count of +1 if over 13 cards have been seen and counted.

CHART NO. 46

Playing the Hard Double Downs
With The One Deck Braun System

DEALER SHOWS

YOU HAVE	2	3	4	5	6	7	8	9	10	ACE
11	—12	—13	—14	—14	—15	—9	—6	—5	—5	—2
10	—9	—10	—11	—12	—13	—7	—4	—2	3	3
9	2	—1	—3	—5	—5	3	8			
8*		11	6	3	3	14				
7			12	8	10					
4,2				11						
3,2				12						

Double down if your count per deck is higher than the value shown. Do not double down if there is no entry.

*For a holding of 4,4 see the comment under the pair splitting tables ahead.

As discussed in conjunction with the 4 deck system you may want to avoid using certain "smart" plays such as doubling on less than 8.

CHART NO. 47

Playing the Soft Double Downs with
The Braun One Deck Count System

DEALER SHOWS

YOU HAVE	2	3	4	5	6	7	8	9	10	ACE
A,10*	14	14	10	8	8	S				
A,9	11	10	7	5	4	15				
A,8	11	4	2	1	0	14				
A,7	2	—2	—15	—14	D	14				
A,6	—1	—7	—12	D	D	8				
A,5	H	5	—5	—10	D	H				
A,4	H	5	—8	—12	—14	H				
A,3	15	5	—3	—8	—9	H				
A,2	10	5	1	—4	—6	H				

Double down if your count per deck exceeds the value in the table; otherwise use basic strategy.

When doubling down on a soft hand is not permitted and for situations not shown in the table use basic strategy. EXCEPTION: Holding soft 18 versus a dealer ace hit if the count per deck is less than —3; otherwise stand.

*The A,10 is not a blackjack. These values are to be used for possibly doubling down on an A,10 resulting from obtaining an ace on a ten after splitting tens.

CHART NO. 48

SPLITTING PAIRS WITH
THE BRAUN ONE DECK COUNT SYSTEM

Doubling Down not permitted after pair splitting

DEALER SHOWS

YOU HAVE	2	3	4	5	6	7	8	9	10	ACE
A,A	SP	SP	SP	SP	SP	SP	—15	—15	—14	—9
10,10	10	8	5	3	4	12				
9,9	0	—4	—4	—7	—7	8	—8	—12		5
8,8	SP	SP	SP	SP	SP	SP	SP	SP	10*	—11
7,7	—10	—11	—14	—16	SP	SP				
6,6	1	—2	—4	—7	—13					
3,3	5	0	—6	—7	SP					
2,2	8	2	—3	—6	—13	SP				

CHART NO. 49

Doubling Down IS permitted after pair splitting

DEALER SHOWS

YOU HAVE	2	3	4	5	6	7	8	9	10	ACE
A,A	SP	SP	SP	SP	SP	SP	—15	—15	—14	—9
10,10	10	8	5	3	4	12				
9,9	—2	—5	—6	—8	—9	4	SP	—12		4
8,8	SP	SP	SP	SP	SP	SP	SP	SP	13*	—11
7,7	SP	SP	SP	SP	SP	SP	SP			
6,6	—1	—4	—7	—10	SP	SP				
4,4		7	2	—3	—2					
3,3	—4	—9	—12	—13	SP	SP				
2,2	—3	—5	—8	—9	—13	SP				

Split if your count per deck equals or exceeds the number shown. Never split 5's. Do not split where there is no entry in the table. Do not split 4's if doubling down is not permitted after splitting; in this case double down if the count is high enough. If doubling down is permitted after splitting, split 4's against a dealer 3, 4, 5, and 6 if the count per deck equals or exceeds the number shown.

*Holding 8,8 versus a dealer 10, split only if the count per deck is less than the value shown.

CHART NO. 50

Late Surrendering with the Braun One Deck Count System

YOU HAVE	2	3	4	5	6	7	8	9	10	ACE
10,7							15	13	11	
9,8							12			
10,6						16	8	2	−2	−1 to 16
9,7						16	8	2	−3	0 to 11
8,8								16	7	
10,5						11	6	2	−1	0
9,6						12	7	3	−2	1 to 12
8,7						16	11	5	1	4 to 10
10,4							14	9	4	4
9,5						13	14	9	5	6
8,6						13	13	7	3	5 to 11
7,7							6*	2	−3	0 to 9
10,3									12	
9,4									13	
8,5							9	10	5	
7,6							8	8	5	
10,2										
9,3								11	12	
8,4								11	12	
7,5								12	14	
6,6								14	15	

If your count per deck is greater than the table entry it pays to surrender the hand. Where the word "to" appears you should surrender if the count per deck is between the values shown. If the table entry is blank you should not surrender, playing the hand according to the usual strategy.

*Holding 7,7 versus dealer 8 you surrender if the count per deck is greater than 6 if doubling is not permitted after splitting. If doubling is permitted after splitting than you surrender if the count per deck is greater than 15.

(Above table covers all counts per deck from −16 to +16)

THE TWO DECK GAME

Nowadays serious professionals infrequently find good one deck games to play - the deck is shuffled too often just when the count gets good. In four deck games they often have quite a wait before the shoe gets to be suitably favorable. The two deck game represents a happy medium. There are quite a few two deck games to be found among the casinos in Las Vegas.

I have not worked out the indexes for my count system for the two deck game. In general, the correct indexes for the two deck games are very nearly half way between those for the one and four deck games.

FIVE AND SIX DECK GAMES

Yes, some casinos are using more than four decks for some or all of their games. This to me seems a greedy grab - these games are tougher to beat. I would stay away from such games unless they have quite liberal rules.

18

OTHER BLACKJACK SYSTEMS

There are quite a number of other systems available. Some are very good. Others are not worth very much, to be perfectly frank. I shall begin with some historical background. This will be followed by my evaluation of several of the principal systems being offered.

The first count system published was Thorp's ten count system in 1962. To develop this system, Thorp ran his computer program for different compositions of the card deck involving different degrees of ten — richness. The use of Thorp's system required keeping track of how many tens and others remained in the deck and computing the ratio of these two counts. From the earlier discussion of insurance it follows that if the ratio of others to tens exceeds 2.0 that insurance is a good bet. Thorp's system provides optimum insurance betting, a reasonable indication of the player's edge and significant improvements in playing strategy in many cases.

Because of the complexity of using Thorp's system a number of authors developed and published simplifications of the ten count system. In general, these simplifications are not as accurate and so do not perform as well as the original. By performance I mean the result "if played perfectly." Accordingly, using one of the simplifications may give up some accuracy, but may gain in ease of use. Noted simplifications are contained in Jacques Noir's *Casino Holiday* published in 1968 by the Oxford Street Press, John Archer's *The Archer Method of Winning at 21* published in 1973 by Henry Regnery Co., and Stanley Roberts' *Winning Blackjack* published in 1971 by Scientific Research Services.

In the first edition of Thorp's *Beat the Dealer*, he proposed a rather complex system called the "ultimate strategy." In this system each card has a point value as follows:

Card:	2	3	4	5	6	7	8	9	10	Ace
Value	5	6	8	11	6	4	0	-3	-7	-9

Starting with a zero count when the cards are shuffled you would add to your count the value of each card as it was seen. This is called the running count. Since the card values are in approximate proportion to their effect on the player's edge as they are removed from the deck, the running count provides an indication of how to vary the bet. However, to optimize the bet size, requires that the count be "normalized." If you have a count of 10 points at the half deck level this is much better than a count of 10 points near the top of the deck. Thorp suggested normalizing by dividing the running count by the number of cards remaining. A simpler method which many like to use is the "count per deck." Yet another idea is to use "count per half deck." Thus, a count of 5 at the half deck level is equivalent to a count of 10 at the full deck level since both are equivalent to a count of 5 per half deck.

Thorp's ultimate strategy required the player to use the normalized count only to determine the size of the bet. For playing the hands the player was to use the ten count strategy. It is a rare individual indeed, who can accurately keep an ultimate index count and ten count at the same time. Possibly a team of two might handle this effectively, but it may not always be feasible to play as a team. Accordingly, the idea developed that one should keep a point count evaluation of the deck and play a strategy relative to this count.

One of the first of the simple count systems to be proposed was the "High-Low" count suggested by Harvey Dubner in 1963. He counted 2's through 6's as +1 point and the tens and aces minus one point each as they are seen. Mr. Dubner used the High-Low primarily for bet variation. He also constructed a crude table of playing indexes mostly by guesswork as he lacked the computer facilities and programming necessary to accurately develop the system. I was impressed with the potential of this system and developed it into a well structured strategy which is published in the second edition of Thorp's book. Since I developed the improved strategy the system is sometimes referred to as the "Braun Point Count." Owing to its appearance in Thorp's book it has also been called the "Thorp Point Count." Shortly after the second edition of Thorp's *Beat the Dealer* appeared I realized I had made a slight error in developing the system. In order to analyze a rich deck situation, for example, the results were calculated after removing one each of the 2's through 6's from the deck leaving all the other cards in the deck to be shuffled. Offhand, this seemed reasonable. Further reflection shows that there is an error in this approach. Since the 7's, 8's, and 9's are not counted in the simple high-low point count system, it follows that on the average each of these cards should constitute about 1/13 of the deck. However, in the depleted decks no 7's, 8's, or 9's were removed; the analysis was made for overly 7, 8, 9 rich decks. Accordingly, this distorted the tables for the playing strategies somewhat. In 1967 I reran the entire analysis with the above error corrected. I did this for both the single and four deck versions of the game but until now my results have not been published.

In the second edition of Thorp's book the point count system, as presented, is shown only for the single deck game. The indexes are presented on a percentage basis, that is, the running count is divided by the number of cards remaining and multiplied by 100%. As you know, in the last chapter we used the concept of count per deck. This does not change the results, but should be simpler to use. Incidentally, slight errors in computing the indexes are of little consequence — I found that correcting the indexes for the single deck game improved results by less than .05%. Independent of my work, Stanford Wong developed indexes for the High-Low system which may be found in his book *Professional Blackjack* published by GBC Press. I disagree with a few of Wong's indexes but in general, his results are close enough.

Over the years many different point count systems have been developed. One noted producer of winning blackjack systems was Lawrence Revere of Las Vegas, Nevada. This was the pseudonym of Leonard or Speck Parsons as the name by which most of his close friends and associates knew him. Upon his death in 1977 it was revealed that Parsons was an alias and that his real name was Griffith K. Owens. Revere published some of his systems in his book *Playing Blackjack as a Business* and also sold a number of systems privately. It is sometimes erroneously stated that I developed Revere's system. Let me set the record straight. Revere used my computer programs which only provided data. The usage of this data and the development of the actual systems was Revere's own work. In some cases he did not develop his systems as accurately as he might have. A number of Revere's systems are reviewed later in this chapter.

Instead of using a point count strategy in which an ace that has been played out of the deck counts a negative number of points it has occurred to some people that it might be better to count the ace as zero points for most purposes in playing the hand owing to the bi-valued nature of this card. As a further refinement, a side ace count may be kept to help determine the bet level and for use in strategy decisions where the number of available aces is an important factor. Some of the strategies reviewed here use this idea.

Although Thorp's ten count system was not designed as a point count system it can be readily converted to that form by counting the tens as minus 9 points each and all the other cards as plus 4 points as they are seen. Now define the count per deck, "C", to be equal to the running count divided by the number of decks remaining, or equivalently,

$$C = \text{RUNNING COUNT} \div (N/52).$$

where N is the number of cards remaining unseen. In Thorp's book the playing indexes are presented as ten count ratio values which I shall call R. To convert the R indexes in Thorp's book to C indexes it follows that

$$C = 52 \times (9 - 4R)/(1 + R).$$

For example, in the ten count system insurance is merited if the ratio of others to tens is *less* than 2. Thus, $C = 52 \times (9 - 4 \times 2)/(1 + 2) = 17\ 1/3$. Therefore, in the ten count point system you should insure if the count per deck *exceeds* 17 1/3. This applies regardless of the number of decks used to play the game.

In general, point count systems balance to zero. That is, at the top of the pack the count is zero and if you add up the values of all the cards you will get zero. As you go through the pack of cards there will typically be positive running counts representing when you generally have the edge, and negative running counts representing when the casino generally has the edge. If all the cards are dealt out the count returns to zero. Thus, to practice a count you might try going through a pack of cards counting as fast as you can. If the count comes out zero, fine! If not, keep practicing!

Jacques Noir, (French for ''Jack Black''!) mentioned earlier, is actually a professor at the University of California in Berkeley. He used an imbalanced point count simplification for the ten count system by assigning a minus 2 for the tens and +1 for the others. His system, its results, and some comparative data on the Ultimate System may be found in his book.

A few years ago I developed a simulation program designed to analyze any balanced point count system to determine its performance. Except for the ''Braun + −,'' which was described in detail in the last chapter, we omit here a description of the strategies employed, but describe in tabular form the point counts used in the systems analyzed.

148

SYSTEM/CARD:	2	3	4	5	6	7	8	9	T	A
BRAUN + —	1	1	1	1	1	0	0	0	-1	-1
REVERE PT. CT.	1	2	2	2	2	1	0	0	-2	-2
REVERE ADVANCED + —	1	1	1	1	1	0	0	-1	-1	0
REVERE ADV PT CT—71	2	3	3	4	3	2	0	-1	-3	-4
REVERE ADV PT CT—73	2	2	3	4	2	1	0	-2	-3	0
GORDON + —	1	1	1	1	0	0	0	0	-1	0
TEN COUNT	4	4	4	4	4	4	4	4	-9	4
EINSTEIN, HI-OPT	0	1	1	1	1	0	0	0	-1	0

The results of the simulation are shown on the next page. All of the simulations were made for runs on one million starting hands. Owing to pair splitting, somewhat more than one million hands were actually played for each simulation run. All of the runs were for single player against the dealer — what is often referred to as "head to head" play. Although the complete printout showed results for bet variations from 1-1 to 1-10 we show here only the 1-1, 1-4, and 1-8 as being sufficiently indicative for comparison purposes. Although each run was made individually the same shuffled decks were used to make the data reasonably comparable. In a run of one million hands the standard deviation of the observed expectation is on the order of 0.1%; however, by using the same shuffled decks the results of the various strategies should be comparable with a quite small error.

The "Basic Braun + —" represents the playing of the hands with basic strategy but using the Dubner Hi-Lo count for bet variation. It will be noted that the gain for flat bets is in approximate agreement with the previously calculated results in Thorp's book, given as .13%. With the addition of about .1% for insurance, which was included, this projects to a figure in accordance with the .2% observed.

STRATEGY	DOUBLE DOWN AFTER SPLIT	SHUFFLE POINT	% OF HANDS AT HIGH BET	% GAIN USING FLAT	1—4	1—8
Part 1—Runs made for 1 deck						
BASIC BRAUN + — 1D	N	.75	21	.2	1.4	2.1
REVERE PT. CT. 1D	N	.75	21	.6	2.1	2.8
REVERE ADV. + — 1D	N	.75	22	.5	1.6	2.2
BRAUN + — 1D	N	.75	21	.7	2.0	2.8
BRAUN + — 4D	N	.75	20½	.6	2.0	2.7
BRAUN + — 4D	Y	.75	20½	.7	2.1	2.9
GORDON + — 4D	Y	.75	20	.7	2.0	2.7
REVERE ADV. PT. CT. — 71 1D	N	.75	22	.6	2.0	2.7
REVERE ADV. PT. CT. — 73 1D	N	.75	21	.8	2.1	2.8
THORP TEN COUNT 1D	Y	.75	20	.7	1.9	2.5
EINSTEIN 1D	N	.75	20	.3	1.5	2.1
HI—OPT 1D	N	.75	20	.8	2.1	2.8
HI-OPT 1D	Y	.75	20	.85	2.2	3.0
Part 2—Runs made for 4 decks						
BRAUN + — 4D	N	.80	12	—.2	0.5	1.1
BRAUN + — 4D	Y	.80	12	—.2	0.7	1.4
GORDON + — 4D	Y	.80	12	—.2	0.7	1.4
REVERE PT. CT. 1D	N	.80	12½	—.3	0.5	1.0
BRAUN + — 1D	N	.80	12	—.3	0.5	1.1
THORP TEN COUNT 1D	Y	.80	11	—.3	0.5	1.0
THORP TEN COUNT 1D	N	.80	11	—.3e	0.3e	0.7e

e = estimated
value, not simulated.

1D = 1 deck strategy

4D = 4 deck strategy

The Revere point count reviewed here is published in his book. The Revere advanced plus minus strategy was sold privately by Revere for $25.00. This was the system, as evaluated. For another $50 Revere provided a more complete set of indexes which improved its performance. The 1971 edition of the Revere advanced point count was sold privately for $200.00. It is found to be slightly inferior to the Revere point count. This is due, presumably, to a bit of error in its development in which Revere did not use properly depleted decks. With the error corrected it would, we suppose, be slightly better. The 1973 edition of the Revere advanced point count was also sold privately for $200.00. Of all the systems reviewed here this was found to be one of the best systems in terms of results achieved. However, it is relatively difficult to use accurately.

The Gordon strategy was developed by Edward Gordon of the Claremont Graduate School and was published in January 1973 by the Claremont Colleges under the title *"Optimum Strategy in Blackjack — A New Analysis"* Economic paper Number 52. The paper was presented at the First Annual Conference on Gambling at the Sahara Hotel in Las Vegas, Nevada in June, 1974. Gordon developed his strategy on the basis of an infinite deck approximation and tested it for the four deck game. The results here show it to be a quite useful strategy for both the four deck and single deck games. Although observed to be slightly inferior to some of the other strategies reviewed here in terms of results at the 1-4 level, some practitioners may find it easier to employ. It is believed that if the Gordon strategy were employed with a separate ace count to better evaluate bet variation and close decisions involving the doubling down on a ten total or nine total that the results would be improved by about .2% on a 1-4 bet variation in the single deck game. Subsequently, various forms of the Gordon system were marketed using as a name, the D.H.M. or D. Howard Miller system.

In 1968 Charles Einstein wrote a book *How to Win at Blackjack* in which he proposed keeping a count of the number of 3's, 4's, 5's, and 6's seen and also a count of the number of tens seen. In 1973, Dr. Peter Griffin of California State University, Sacramento, California examined this count and deduced that if it were properly parameterized that it would be an excellent count. Dr. Edward O. Thorp has independently confirmed this. To the best of this writer's knowledge this count was original with Mr. Einstein and he is to be congratulated for his insight in picking this count as recent research revealed that optimum playing results for a simple plus one, minus one count system are achieved by an optimized system based on this count. Lawrence Revere was sufficiently impressed by Einstein's work to some years ago develop his own version of the 3-4-5-6 versus tens count systems, but unfortunately, he failed to realize how powerful it was and discarded it in favor of his other systems. Revere's version was better than Einstein's, but inferior to the completely optimized version. Mr. Einstein produced a good system in 1968, but it lacked many refinements, and had some errors in its strategy tables. With the aid of Braun's computer programs the optimization was done in 1974 by a Mr. G. under contract to International Gaming, Inc., Thornhill, Ontario. The strategy tables were independently derived and the resultant system was given the name HI-OPT. A substantial improvement in results over the earlier Einstein system was achieved as can be seen in the table of comparative performances presented earlier.

Near the end of Einstein's book there is presented a test of 2580 hands with a gain of 4.8% with a 1-3-5 betting system. This shows what could happen in a relatively short run, but it should not be regarded as representative.* Such a result or better will happen from time to time — a "lucky" run. To establish the long term results of a system with a reasonable degree of accuracy requires a much longer test. To compare Einstein's system to the others previously compared we programmed his system for playing the hands just as stated in his book. This involved leaving the running count as is, for there is no provision for adjusting the count relative to the deck level (except for one instance: figure 11, rule B in his book). We then played 1,000,000 hands using the same shuffled decks as we did for the previous systems dealt down to the 3/4 deck level, as before. To make the results comparable to the Hi-opt we used the Hi-opt rules for increasing the bet and for insurance which are more accurate than the Einstein System. Therefore, the only difference in the computer run was the playing strategy.

Some runs have been made using a four deck strategy in a single deck game and a single deck strategy in a four deck game. The loss in applying a strategy developed for a certain number of decks to a game with a different number of decks as compared to applying the appropriate strategy for the specified number of decks appears to be small.

The advantage of the count player will increase sharply as the end of the deck is approached. For this reason the casinos generally shuffle well before the deck runs out. We tested the Gordon strategy in a one deck game with a shuffle point of .8 instead of .75 and used count per deck of

*Einstein himself indicates that the test was not exhaustive.

153

2.0 to increase the bet. This reduced the percent of hands at the high bet level to 17% but nevertheless increased the player's gain to 2.2% for a 1-4 bet, 3.0% for 1-8. We also tried the Gordon strategy in a 4 deck game dealt to the 90% level with 13½ % of the hands at the high bet. This resulted in a 1.1% gain for a 1-4 bet, 1.8% for 1-8.

In all of the systems in which the ace counts zero no attempt was made to evaluate the ensuing results if the player were to keep a side ace count to better evaluate his bet size. In addition a side ace count would be useful in close decisions involving the doubling down on a 10 or 9 total. With the addition of this feature the player ought to gain an estimated additional 0.2% on a 2-4 bet variation. Also doubling down after pair splitting is worth an additional 0.1% at the 1-4 level; accordingly, both the Hi-opt and the Revere advanced point count -73% employed with these features in a single deck game dealt to the 75% level in head to head play would yield about 2.4% to the player accurately employing the system.

The two top performing systems reviewed here are the Revere Advanced Point Count, 1973 version and the Hi-opt. In view of the much simpler count in the Hi-opt it is surprising that it performs as well. There appears to be a point of limited returns and superstructuring the count does not necessarily lead to an overall improvement. In actuality the Revere system with *complete* optimization would perform slightly better than the Hi-opt. We doubt that the additional gain would be worth the mental effort of using the more complex count.

In a few Nevada casinos the player is allowed to throw in his two card starting hand giving up half his bet. If the dealer has an ace or ten showing this *surrender* play can only be done after the dealer ascertains that he is not holding a blackjack. In Thorp's book it is stated that the basic strategy (i.e., without counting) for surrender would result in a gain of 0.15%. This was computed on the assumption that the player could throw in any hand at any time which was believed to be the way the surrender option was at one time played in Macao and Manila where it is believed to have originated. With the more restrictive rules currently employed in the few Nevada casinos where late surrender is available the gain for a noncount player is only about .02% in the single deck game and .06% in the four deck game. For a count player the gain can, of course, be more substantial. The point count simulation program was modified to allow for the possibility of surrender and the Hi-opt surrender strategy table was programmed and tested. It was found that for the surrendered hands that, if they had been played out, an average loss of 53.5% would have occurred. Thus, surrender resulted in an average saving of 3.3% for the hands involved. It was found that about 2 out of 55 hands should be surrendered. Now 2/55 of 3.3% = .12%, which is the gain on a flat bet for the count player. On a 1-4 betting scale surrender was found to yield a gain of .25%.

There are some blackjack systems being offered in which it is claimed to be unnecessary to count the cards. Such systems are generally of the same ilk as craps and roulette systems. Without counting the cards a long run gain of only about .1% to .2% with the most favorable rules can be expected. Thus, to achieve a worthwhile gain is apt to require the effort of using some count system. Adjustment of the running count for the deck level is an additional, but desirable chore, to obtain optimized results with an upper practical limit of about .9% for a flat bet in a single deck game dealt to the 3/4 level (13 or less cards remaining).

Some systems have been derived which are quite near this upper practical limit mentioned. Two such systems are the Hi-Opt II and the Uston Advanced Point Count System. The point count values are as shown:

Card:	2	3	4	5	6	7	8	9	10	A
Hi-Opt II	1	1	2	2	1	1	0	0	-2	0
Uston	1	2	2	3	2	2	2	-1	-3	0

The Hi-Opt II was developed in 1976. It is available from the same source as the Hi-Opt. Ken Uston achieved some fame with his book *The Big Player* and his suits against various casinos for harrassment and improper barring. Wanting to have a system with his name on it, he commissioned some mathematically talented programmers at one of the western universities to work out the system for the indicated count. It performs about as well as the Hi-Opt II, but it is comparatively difficult to accurately use. Uston's system may be obtained from the Uston Institute of Blackjack.

Prices of blackjack systems vary from the cost of a book up to about $200. If you decide to pursue a count strategy I don't think the price should be the determining factor. As long as it's a good strategy, relative ease of use should be an important consideration. I would therefore recommend my strategies in the previous chapter (of course!) or the Hi Opt strategy. A bit more difficult, but also recommended are the Hi Opt II and the Revere point count in his book. When you go to systems that use counts up to plus or minus three or more I believe the small additional potential gain, if any, will not be worth pursuing. Knowledgeable professionals find it not worth the effort and sometimes lose count. Most professionals use one of the simpler counts.

If you do become proficient at using one of the count systems and if you vary your bet too much the casinos may bar you from further play. There are numerous suggestions for how to handle yourself in the casinos to avoid getting barred. Wong generally advises a table hopping procedure in which you do not play much against unfavorable decks. Skillful psychology can often be employed. A most interesting account of this can be found in Ian Anderson's *Turning the Tables on Las Vegas* published in 1976.

NOTE: For additional information on HI-OPT, see Carl Cooper and Lance Humble's new Blackjack book published by Doubleday, 1980.

19

THE DEALER'S "HOLE CARD EXPOSED" BLACKJACK

About 20 to 25 years ago, personnel in many Nevada Casinos believed the Casinos would still have an advantage even if the dealer's hole card was exposed. A proposition game on this basis was arranged at the Flamingo Casino by one astute player. However, the game was called off after the player had won several thousand dollars. Amazingly, a casino in Winnemucca, Nevada regularly dealt such a game but only allowed a $10 bet limit.

Approximately 17 years ago, I computed the player's edge to be about 9.9% in a typical Las Vegas Strip one deck game, if the player always knew the dealer's hole card and played optimally with this knowledge. My data for this game's strategy was presented in the second edition of Edward Thorp's *Beat The Dealer* and also in Richard Epstein's *Theory of Gambling and Statistical Logic.*

This information was of some use even in a game where the dealer's hole card was not exposed, because, in those days, the deck was frequently dealt out to the end. Thus, when the deck ran out and the dealer had to re-shuffle after having received his hole card, an expert card counter would know the dealer's hole card and could play such hands accordingly. Also, on occasion the dealer's hole card might be inadvertently or (in some cases) deliberately exposed. However, these days one should not regularly expect such Casino generosity.

Then, I asked myself — what if a Casino permitted the dealer to regularly show his hole card but, to make the game more fair, the dealer would win all ties? I found the knowledgable player would still win at a 2.1% rate. My data for this computation was presented in Epstein's book. Incidentally, Epstein coined a name for this game — "Zweikartenspiel" — German for "two card play".

In October 1979, Vegas World decided to introduce this game with several rules modifications which would give the edge back to the Casino. Bob Stupak of Vegas World copyrighted the name "Double Exposure 21" for his version of this game. Presumably, several other Casinos which have introduced this game will be unable to use this copyrighted name and will call it something else, such as "No Secrets Blackjack" or "Naked 21", etc.

As of April 1980, Dealer's "Hole Card Exposed" Blackjack was being played at nine Casinos in and around Las Vegas. The rules in effect at Vegas World for "Double Exposure 21" were as follows:

- *Five decks of cards are used.*
- *The player always wins with a Blackjack but he wins EVEN MONEY instead of 3 to 2. However, an Ace of Spades with a Jack of Spades PAYS DOUBLE.*
- *Except for Blackjack, DEALER WINS ALL TIES.*
- *Double down on any two cards except after pair splitting.*
- *Dealer hits soft 17.*
- *A total of 21 achieved with 6, 7, and 8 of the same suit PAYS DOUBLE.*

With these rules and optimum basic strategy play, I estimate the player is at a .5% disadvantage. The basic strategy for 5 deck "Double Exposure 21" is summarized in the following chart.

"Double Exposure 21" is copyrighted by Vegas World 1979.

Basic Strategy for 5 Deck "Double Exposure 21"*

DEALER'S 2 CARD TOTAL	DOUBLE-DOWNS HARD	DOUBLE-DOWNS SOFT	SPLIT PAIRS	HARD STAND AT OR ABOVE	SOFT STAND AT OR ABOVE
4	10,11	18	A,6-9	12	18
5	9-11	16-18	A-3,6-9	12	18
6	9-11	13-18	A-3,6-9	12	18
7	10,11		A,8	16 or 17**	18
8	10,11		A,8,9	16	19
9	11		A	16	19
10			A	15	19
11				14	18
12	8-11	13-19	A-4,6-9	12	18
13	8-11	13-20	A-4,6-10	12	18
14	5-11	13-20	A-4,6-10	12	18
15	5-11	13-20	A-4,6-10	12	18
16	5-11	13-20	A-4,6-10	12	18
17			2,3,6-8	18	18
18			9	19	19
19				20	20
20				21	21
Soft 12			A	13	19
Soft 13	11		A	13	19
Soft 14	10,11		A	12	19
Soft 15	10,11		A,9	12	19
Soft 16	10,11		A,8,9	12	19
Soft 17			A,8	18	18
Soft 18				19	19
Soft 19				20	20
Soft 20				21	21

**There is very little difference in this case. Hit the 9,7 hard 16 versus dealer total of 7 for a very slight gain. Stand on other hard "16's," except the 8,8 which should be split. EXCEPTION: If you get an 8 on a split 8, hit it.)

EPILOG

LUCK AND SKILL

I have always been intrigued by the interplay between luck and skill, particularly as they relate to Blackjack. In this relationship, I define skill as the ability to put into effective use all of the information contained in the previous chapters.

There is no real secret to becoming a skillful Blackjack player. As we discussed in our chapter on Practice, and as in anything you wish to do well, you must continually apply yourself to achieve total familiarity and perception. Think of things you now do well. How did it happen? Even if you show an inclination toward that type of thing, you might be surprised by adding up the number of hours and days you have worked to achieve your present superiority.

For those of you to whom figures do not come easy, it just means you have to work a little longer than others. But if your goal is to become a good Blackjack player, so it must be.

As for luck, that's quite another thing. One dictionary defines it this way, "la; a force that brings good fortune or adversity; b: the events or circumstances which operate for or against an individual; 2; favoring chance."

As synonyms, we have words like "fortunate," "providential," "fate." I have always had trouble with such words. For example, take the word 'providential'. Surely that suggests, or at least implies, the help or intervention of some higher power. Frankly, I'm not about to touch that one.

It has been said that to a sensible man there is no such thing as chance. Or as Voltaire put it, "Chance is a word void of sense; nothing can exist without a cause."

Both of these reinforce the idea of odds and of computer determined probabilities. On the other hand, I can not entirely dismiss the idea of "luck."

How often have you seen a player who can seem to do no wrong? That player will pull 5's to his sixteens and 8's to his thirteens. On the other side of the table are the Dealers, some of whom are busting or some who also can do no wrong. It is said of such a Dealer that he or she is "hot."

My own way of coming to terms with some of these phenomena is to introduce the word "cycles," that which is uninterrupted or linear, and which I might add, can very quickly be interrupted and become nonlinear.

With all of this said, I re-confirm my belief in probabilities, and therefore in skill. Do the two ideas necessarily conflict? I say no. Skill can only be enhanced by good fortune. In fact, the best of all worlds is to have a skillful player get lucky.

And that, dear reader, is what I wish you. Develop your skills, and trust them...and as Cervantes has said, "When good luck comes to thee, take it in."

We hope you have enjoyed reading Julian Braun's "How to Play Winning Blackjack". It will continue to serve you as an invaluable reference book for years to come.

Additional copies may be ordered by writing us at Data House Publishing Co., 7525 No. Wolcott Avenue, Chicago, IL 60626.

We will be happy to assist you in the procurement of any of the books or systems mentioned, as well as in any questions you may have. Feel free to write us.

The Publisher

GLOSSARY OF TERMS

BUST   When total count of the cards is over 21.

DOUBLE DOWN   The act of doubling your wager after receiving your first two cards and then receiving one card face down. Some casinos permit doubling down on any two cards. Others are more restrictive.

HARD COUNT   The total value of your cards in which Aces are either not present, or if present, are counted as 1.

HIT   Signifies your desire for an additional card.

HOLE CARD   Usually signifies the Dealer's concealed card.

INSURANCE   The rule of allowing you to "bet" half your wager that the Dealer has a blackjack. Allowed only when the Dealer has an Ace as his up card.

PUSH   The result of a tie count between yourself and the Dealer. No one wins.

SHOE   The plastic container used by the Dealer to hold the cards when playing Blackjack with 4 or more decks.

SOFT COUNT   The total value of your cards when they contain an Ace, counted as 11.

SPLITTING PAIRS The rule whereby you can split two similar cards such as two eights and play them as separate hands.

STAND OR STAY   Means you are satisfied with you count, and do not wish any additional cards.

STIFF	Generally, a hand containing a hard count of 12 to 16.
SURRENDER	The rule allowing you to give up on a hand which you do not believe has much of a chance and only losing half of your bet.
EARLY SURRENDER	The rule allowing you to relinquish your hand and give up half your bet when the dealer is showing an Ace or ten before the dealer has looked at (or received) his hole card.
FIVE CARD SURRENDER	The rule allowing you to automatically win half your bet with a 5 card hand not exceeding 21 to avoid the risk of the hand being tied or beaten. Generally available only in the Far East casinos.

BASIC STRATEGY

TEST A

YOUR CARDS	DEALER SHOWS	STRATEGY	✔ OR X
9,9	4		
12	6		
4,4	2		
A,A	3		
10	4		
9	7		
14	2		
7,7	6		
A,4	4		
4,4	6		
10	9		
6,6	4		
A,8	9		
11	9		
2,2	3		

YOUR CARDS	DEALER SHOWS	STRATEGY	✔ OR X
13	8		
A,8	5		
3,3	6		
A,7	2		
13	4		
6,6	4		
15	3		
2,2	2		
6,5	7		
A,4	6		
A,7	9		
3,3	4		
9,9	A		
4,4	7		
A,4	3		

H	S	D	SP	G
		Double	Split	Surrender
Hit	Stand	Down	Pairs	(Give Up)

168

BASIC STRATEGY

B

TEST B

YOUR CARDS	DEALER SHOWS	STRATEGY	✓ OR X
13	2		
3,3	3		
5,3	6		
9,9	4		
7,7	4		
6,3	5		
9	7		
A,3	4		
7,7	8		
A,7	6		
9,9	A		
A,3	4		
9,9	3		
A,5	3		
6,6	3		

YOUR CARDS	DEALER SHOWS	STRATEGY	✓ OR X
A,3	3		
6,3	4		
A,8	2		
7,7	5		
7,2	7		
2,2	5		
6,6	6		
A,8	5		
13	8		
2,2	4		
15	2		
6,6	2		
2,2	7		
4,4	2		
A,6	2		

H	S	D	SP	G
		Double	Split	Surrender
Hit	Stand	Down	Pairs	(Give Up)

169

BASIC STRATEGY

TEST C

YOUR CARDS	DEALER SHOWS	STRATEGY	✓ OR X
4,4	4		
3,3	8		
A,2	4		
12	2		
A,7	10		
9,9	A		
A,9	5		
9,2	8		
15	A		
A,3	5		
2,2	3		
A,6	5		
14	3		
7,2	6		
12	4		

YOUR CARDS	DEALER SHOWS	STRATEGY	✓ OR X
A,6	2		
9,9	5		
8,8	9		
A,6	5		
7,2	9		
A,6	5		
A,7	A		
15	2		
A,4	3		
9,9	9		
8,8	10		
A,2	4		
10	4		
4,4	5		
A,6	6		

H	S	D	SP	G
		Double	Split	Surrender
Hit	Stand	Down	Pairs	(Give Up)

170

BASIC STRATEGY

TEST D

YOUR CARDS	DEALER SHOWS	STRATEGY	✓ OR X
6,6	7		
7,7	9		
A,4	4		
A,2	3		
2,2	8		
6,6	8		
A,7	4		
3,3	3		
2,2	2		
A,5	6		
A,7	9		
15	2		
7,7	6		
A,5	4		
A,7	7		

YOUR CARDS	DEALER SHOWS	STRATEGY	✓ OR X
4,4	2		
A,8	3		
6,6	6		
9,9	A		
A,3	5		
2,2	3		
3,3	7		
A,7	6		
7,7	10		
A,7	5		
9,9	6		
A,5	5		
16	7		
17	10		
6,6	4		

H	S	D	SP	G
		Double Down	Split Pairs	Surrender (Give Up)
Hit	Stand			

NOTES: